Chevette 1975-79 Autobook

By the Autobooks Team of Writers and Illustrators

Vauxhall Chevette 1975-76
Vauxhall Chevette E, L 1975-79
Vauxhall Chevette GL, GLS 1976-79

Autobooks Ltd. Golden Lane Brighton BN1 2QJ England

The AUTOBOOK series of Workshop Manuals is the largest in the world and covers the majority of British and Continental motor cars, as well as the majority of Japanese and Australian models.

Whilst every care has been taken to ensure correctness of information it is obviously not possible to guarantee complete freedom from errors or omissions or to accept liability arising from such errors or omissions.

CONTENTS

ISBN 0 85147 938 3

First Edition   1976
Second Edition, fully revised   1978
Third Edition, fully revised   1979

871

Printed in Brighton England for Autobooks Ltd by G. Beard and Son Ltd
Bound in Hove England for Autobooks Ltd by Jilks Ltd

C

INTRODUCTION

This do-it-yourself Workshop Manual has been specially written for the owner who wishes to maintain his vehicle in first class condition and to carry out the bulk of his own servicing and repairs. Considerable savings on garage charges can be made, and one can drive in safety and confidence knowing the work has been done properly.

Comprehensive step-by-step instructions and illustrations are given on most dismantling, overhauling and assembling operations. Certain assemblies require the use of expensive special tools, the purchase of which would be unjustified. In these cases information is included but the reader is recommended to hand the unit to the agent for attention.

Throughout the Manual hints and tips are included which will be found invaluable, and there is an easy to follow fault diagnosis at the end of each chapter.

Whilst every care has been taken to ensure correctness of information it is obviously not possible to guarantee complete freedom from errors or omissions or to accept liability arising from such errors or omissions.

Instructions may refer to the righthand or lefthand sides of the vehicle or the components. These are the same as the righthand or lefthand of an observer standing behind the vehicle and looking forward.

The Chevette GL Hatchback

CHAPTER 1

THE ENGINE

1:1 Description

The engine is a conventional four cylinder in-line unit of 1256cc capacity, with pushrod operated overhead valves.

The cast iron cylinder block is integral with the upper part of the crankcase, the lower half of which is formed by the pressed steel sump. The overhead valves are set in line along the cylinder head and are operated by pressed steel rockers pivoting on ball studs. The rockers are operated from the camshaft by means of tappets and vertical pushrods.

The crankshaft is carried in three main bearings fitted with renewable steel-backed bearing shells, similar shells being fitted at the big-end bearing positions. Crankshaft end float is controlled by flanges on the upper half of the centre main bearing. Spring-loaded oil seals are provided at both ends of the crankshaft. The solid skirt pistons have offset gudgeon pins which are an interference fit in the connecting rods. The three bearing camshaft is driven by a single-row roller chain from the crankshaft, the chain being fitted with an automatic tensioning device.

The crankcase is ventilated through a hose connected between the rocker cover and the carburetter air cleaner, and a hose connected to the inlet manifold.

Lubrication is provided by a gear-type oil pump mounted in the crankcase and driven from the camshaft, the upper end of the pump driving spindle having an offset slot to engage with the distributor shaft. The pump includes a spring-loaded plunger type relief valve. An external fullflow oil filter is mounted on the lefthand side of the engine. Filtered oil is fed to the main oil gallery and through drillings in the cylinder block to the crankshaft. Oil directed through a nozzle within the timing chain tensioner provides hydraulic damping to the tensioner and lubricates the tensioner pad and timing chain. The rocker gear is lubricated from an oil gallery in the cylinder head via drillings in the rocker studs. **FIG 1:1** shows a longitudinal section through the engine assembly.

1:2 Removing the engine

The normal operations of decarbonising and cylinder head servicing can be carried out without the need for engine removal. A major overhaul, however, can only be satisfactorily carried out with the engine removed and

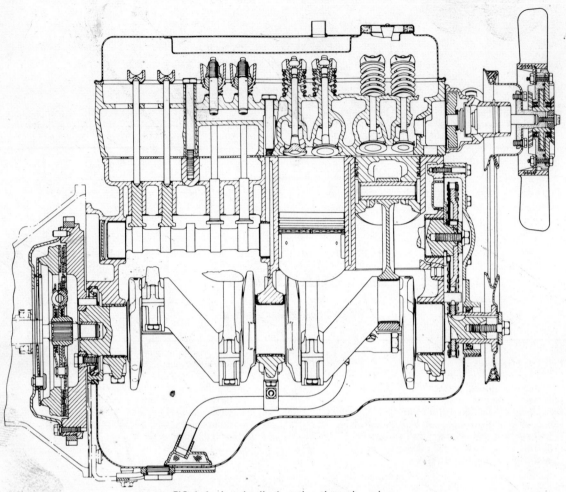

FIG 1:1 Longitudinal section through engine

transferred to the bench. Note that, in the case of an engine needing major overhaul work and, possibly, cylinder reboring, it may well prove to be more economical to fit a complete reconditioned engine. This procedure requires that the original engine is removed, the ancilliary components transferred from it to the reconditioned unit, which is then fitted to the vehicle. This procedure will effect a great saving in labour time and guarantees engine performance.

If the owner is not a skilled motor engineer, it is suggested that he will find much useful information in **Hints on Maintenance and Overhaul** at the end of this manual and that he read it before starting work. It must be stressed that all lifting equipment should be sound and firmly based and not likely to collapse under the weight imposed.

Removal:

Remove the bonnet and disconnect the battery. Drain the oil from the engine sump.

Drain the cooling system, collecting the coolant if it is to be re-used. Remove the radiator as described in **Chapter 4**. Refer to **Chapter 2** and remove the air cleaner, the carburetter controls and the fuel feed pipe. Plug the feed pipe to prevent fuel leakage.

Remove the exhaust pipe from the manifold. Disconnect the engine wiring harness, starter cable and earth strap, making sure that every connection between the engine and bodywork is released. Disconnect the heater hoses from the engine.

Remove the nuts securing the front engine mountings to the front crossmember. Details of a front engine mounting are shown in **FIG 1:2**.

Fit the lifting equipment and take the weight of the engine. Support the front of the gearbox with a suitable jack or stand placed beneath the bellhousing. Disconnect the gearbox brace beneath the sump and remove the bolts securing the gearbox to the crankcase. Move the engine slightly forwards to disengage the gearbox input shaft from the clutch hub, taking great care to avoid imposing any side or vertical loads on the shaft as this could cause serious damage to the clutch unit.

Check that all connections between the engine and car body are free, then lift out the engine.

1:3 Removing and refitting cylinder head

Disconnect the battery earth cable and drain the cooling system, collecting the coolant in a clean container if it is to be re-used. Refer to **FIG 1:35** and disconnect the breather hoses. Remove the air cleaner and carburetter as described in **Chapter 2**. Remove the radiator and heater hoses from the cylinder head. Disconnect the servo vacuum pipe.

Remove the inlet manifold. Disconnect the exhaust pipe. Remove the sparking plugs.

Remove the fan belt as described in **Chapter 4**. Remove the ignition coil. Disconnect the wire from the temperature gauge unit if fitted.

Remove the rocker cover. If the head is to be completely stripped, the rockers may be removed next by undoing their centre nuts. Alternatively, the nuts need only be slackened enough to allow the rockers to be swung round for the pushrods to be removed as shown in **FIG 1:3**. Ensure that each valve is closed before slackening its rocker nut and take care not to drop the pushrod back once it is disengaged from the tappet. Mark the pushrods so that they can be refitted in the same order and the same way up.

Remove the cylinder head bolts, slackening each bolt a little at a time in the reverse order to that shown for tightening in **FIG 1:4**. Lift off the head and gasket. If the head sticks do not try to prise it off with a screwdriver as this may damage the joint faces. Instead, carefully jarr the head free with light blows from a soft-faced hammer.

Refitting:

Thoroughly clean the joint faces of the cylinder head and cylinder block. Position a new cylinder head gasket on the cylinder block, noting that the gasket is marked 'Front' for correct fitting. No jointing compound must be used, it being essential to fit the gasket dry. Refit the cylinder head and fit the retaining bolts finger tight. Tighten the head bolts a little at a time in the order shown in **FIG 1 4**, to a final torque of 55lb ft.

Install the pushrods in the correct order, taking care not to drop them past the tappets into the crankcase. A tight fitting rubber grommet temporarily installed on the top end of the pushrod will prevent this trouble. Refit the rockers. Adjust the valve clearances as described in **Section 1:5**. Refit and adjust the drive belt as described in **Chapter 4**, then reassemble the remaining components in the reverse order of dismantling, but leave the rocker cover off. Refill the cooling system as described in **Chapter 4**, then start the engine and run it until it reaches normal operating temperature. The valve clearances must now be readjusted as described in **Section 1:5**. On completion, refit the rocker cover, using a new gasket and refit the breather hose.

1:4 Servicing the head and valve gear

FIG 1:5 shows the cylinder head components.

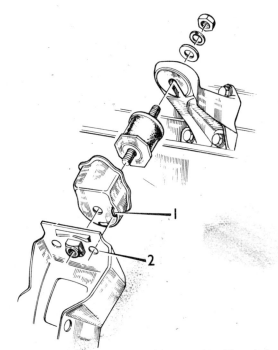

FIG 1:2 Details of front engine mounting. The tab 1 locates in hole 2

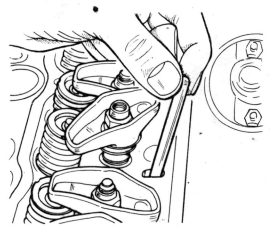

FIG 1:3 Removing a pushrod

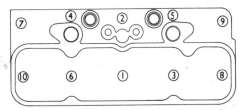

FIG 1:4 Cylinder head bolt tightening sequence. Loosen the bolts in the reverse order to that shown

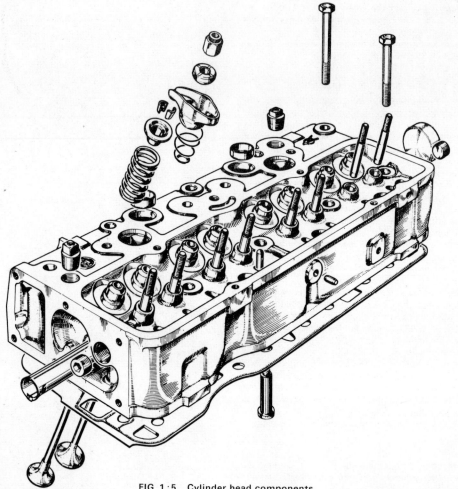

FIG 1:5 Cylinder head components

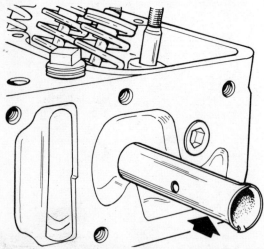

FIG 1:6 Water distributor tube removal

Dismantling:

Remove the exhaust manifold. Remove the water pump, after which the water distributor tube can be withdrawn for cleaning as shown in **FIG 1:6**.

During the dismantling procedure, mark or store all valve gear components in the correct order for refitting in their original positions, if they are not to be renewed.

Remove the rocker adjusting nuts, then remove the rocker balls, rockers and springs. Using a suitable valve spring compressor tool, compress each valve spring in turn and remove the split taper collets. Release the spring compressor and remove the spring cap, spring and valve from the cylinder head. Release the spring clips and remove the stem seals from the inlet valve positions on the cylinder head.

Servicing:

Valves:

When the valves have been cleaned of carbon deposits they must be inspected for serviceability. Valves with bent stems or badly burned heads must be renewed. Valves that are too pitted to clean up on grinding to their seats may be refaced at a garage, but the amount of metal that can be removed in this operation is limited and new valves will be required if refacing cannot be successfully carried out. If the valve head thickness, shown at A in **FIG 1 : 7**, is less than 0.8mm (0.03in) for inlet valves or less than 1.0mm (0.04in) for exhaust valves after refacing, the valve in question must be renewed. Check the valve stem for wear or scoring.

Valve springs:

Test the valve springs by comparison with the figures given in **Technical Data**, or compare their efficiency with that of a new spring. To compare with a new spring, insert both the old and new springs end to end with a metal plate between them into the jaws of a vice or under a press. If the old spring is weakened it will close up first when pressure is applied. Make sure that the load is applied squarely to prevent the springs from flying out under pressure. If any spring is shorter or weaker than standard it must be renewed.

Valve guides:

No separate valve guides are used, the valves operating directly in bores machined in the cylinder head. Guide bores that are worn or scored must be reamed to accept new valves with suitable oversize stems. Four oversizes are available, 0.003, 0.006, 0.010 and 0.012in. The correct reamer sizes are tools Z8548, Z8549, Z8550 or Z8565 respectively. To ensure an accurate bore at the valve port, reaming should be carried out from the top of the cylinder head as shown in **FIG 1 : 8**.

Valve seats:

Valve seats in the cylinder head that are too pitted to clean up on grinding to the valves may be refaced at a garage, to the correct angle of 45°.

Rockers and studs:

Inspect the rockers for wear or damage and renew any found to be unserviceable. Damaged threads on rocker studs can be cleaned up by using a suitable die nut. Check that the rocker balls are a free fit on the stud shanks. The balls must be fitted with the spherical face towards the rocker and the threads and shank of the studs should be smeared with hypoid gear oil to prevent excessive friction.

Inspect the rocker studs to check that none are loose in the cylinder head. Check the fit of the self-locking nuts on the threads. Lubricate the thread with hypoid gear oil and test for a minimum reading with a torque wrench of 3lb ft to turn the nut, when the nut is fully engaged on the thread. If a lower reading is obtained the nut is too slack and may loosen in service. If the stud is in good condition then the fitting of a new nut may overcome the trouble, but if this still gives a reading that is too low the stud must be renewed as well. As this involves extracting the old stud, reaming the hole and pressing in an oversize stud, the work should be entrusted to a fully equipped service station.

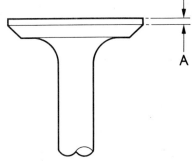

FIG 1 : 7   Check the valve head thickness after refacing, as described in the text

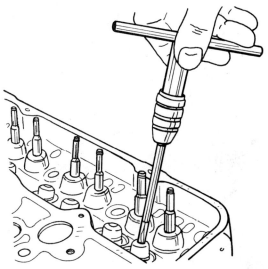

FIG 1 : 8   Reaming valve guide bores to accept valves with oversize stems

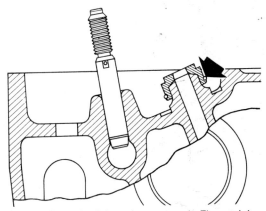

FIG 1 : 9   Installing inlet valve stem seals. The retaining circlip is arrowed

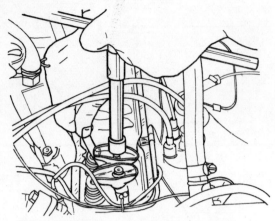

FIG 1:10 Checking and adjusting valve clearances

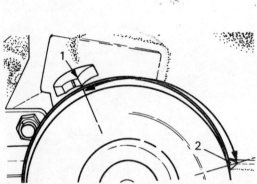

FIG 1:11 Checking valve timing. The method is described in the text

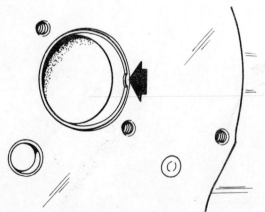

FIG 1:12 Camshaft bearings must be located with the notch towards the front of the crankcase

Decarbonising and valve grinding:

Using suitable tools which will not scratch the metal surfaces, remove all traces of carbon from the combustion chambers, inlet and exhaust ports and joint faces. Plug the water and oilways in the top surface of the cylinder block with pieces of clean rag to prevent the entry of dirt, then clean the carbon from the piston crowns. Take care not to damage the light alloy pistons during this operation.

Grind the valves to their seats, starting with coarse grade and finishing with fine grade carborundum paste, unless the seats are in very good condition when fine grade paste can be used alone. Use a suction type valve grinding tool and work with a semi-rotary movement, lifting the valve clear of its seat occasionally and turning to a different position before continuing. When the seats of both valve and cylinder head show a smooth matt grey finish on their matching faces, grinding is complete. When the work is finished, clean away every trace of grinding paste from the cylinder head, valves and guides.

Reassembly:

This is a reversal of the dismantling procedure. Use hypoid gear oil to lubricate the rocker stud threads, engine oil for all other moving parts. Make sure that the light springs beneath the rockers are fitted with the smaller coils towards the cylinder head. Use new inlet valve stem seals and secure with the circlips, as shown in **FIG 1:9**. Before installing inlet valves, smear the seal lips with oil and remove any burrs on the valve stem grooves to avoid damaging the seals. Use new gaskets when refitting the water pump and exhaust manifold.

1:5 Valve clearance adjustment

Final adjustment to valve clearances must be carried out with the engine at normal operating temperature and running at a slow idle. If the rocker assembly has been removed and replaced, however, the clearance should first be adjusted in the following manner, in order that the engine can be started and tuned.

Remove the rocker cover. Work on one pair of valves at a time and, with the piston at the top of the cylinder on the compression stroke (both valves closed), adjust the valves as shown in **FIG 1:10**. Using a feeler gauge between the rocker and the valve stem, adjust the clearance to 0.2mm (0.008in) at both inlet and exhaust valve positions.

Turn the adjusting nut clockwise to reduce the clearance, or anticlockwise to increase the clearance. The adjusting nut is self-locking. This adjustment is only a temporary measure, and final adjustment must be carried out as follows:

Run the engine to warm it up to normal operating temperature. Stop the engine and remove the rocker cover.

Start the engine and leave it running at slow idle. Insert the feeler gauge as previously described and turn the adjusting nut until the clearance is correct, then remove the spanner and recheck. Leave the feeler gauge between the rocker and valve stem while the rocker is operating and, during the short period that the valve is closed, check that the feeler moves in the gap with a slight drag, being neither tight nor loose.

Refit the rocker cover, using a new gasket. If the head has been removed and a new head gasket fitted, run the engine for about 100 miles then recheck the tightness of the cylinder head bolts and recheck the valve clearances. Every time the cylinder head bolts are tightened it will affect the valve clearances, so always check them afterwards.

1:6 Removing timing gear and camshaft

For this work to be carried out, the engine must be removed from the car as described in **Section 1:2**. However, the valve timing can be checked without the need for engine removal or dismantling.

To check the valve timing, remove the rocker cover and sparking plugs. Refer to **FIG 1:11**. From the centre of the pointer on the crankshaft pulley, mark the pulley rim at a point 117mm (4.60in), measured circumferentially and in an anticlockwise direction. Mount a dial gauge over the inlet valve of No. 1 cylinder (the second valve from the front of the engine) so that its button rests on the valve spring cap. Turn the engine in its normal (clockwise) direction until the gauge shows that the valve is fully open. At this point, the mark made on the pulley should be in line with the TDC pointer 1 on the timing case.

To remove the timing gear and camshaft, remove the engine, then remove the drive belt, fuel pump and distributor. If the head is not to be removed, remove the pushrods as described in **Section 1:3** and lay the engine on its side. If the head is to be removed, do so now and invert the engine.

Remove the sump and oil pump as described in **Section 1:8**. Remove the crankshaft pulley and remove the timing case from the front of the engine. Remove the bolts securing the camshaft sprocket. Withdraw the two sprockets together with the chain. The dowel locating the camshaft sprocket is an interference fit in the sprocket and should come away with it. Remove the camshaft thrust plate. Make sure that the tappets are clear of their respective cams and withdraw the camshaft.

Remove the tappets, keeping them in order so that each can be fitted in its original bore. Remove the timing chain tensioner from the timing case.

1:7 Refitting timing gear and camshaft

Before reassembly, examine all parts and renew any found worn or damaged. Check the camshaft for worn bearing journals and cam lobes and check that the measurement from base to peak of each cam is within the limit given in **Technical Data**. Examine the skew gear. If this is badly worn or damaged, both camshaft and oil pump drive gear must be renewed. Inspect the timing chain and examine both sprockets for worn teeth. If they are badly worn, both sprockets should be renewed together with the chain. Renew any tappets which are worn or pitted on the bottom surface.

Replacement camshaft bearings are supplied with bores finished to size, so that if renewal is required they do not need to be bored in line. Removal and refitting is facilitated by using the special tools available from the manufacturers.

To remove the camshaft bearings the flywheel must be removed. Drive out the front camshaft bearing first,

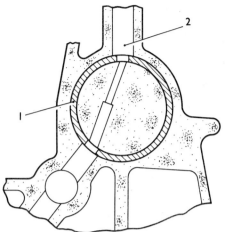

FIG 1:13 Section through camshaft centre bearing showing alignment of oilways

Key to Fig 1:13   1 Bearing   2 Oil feed to rocker gallery

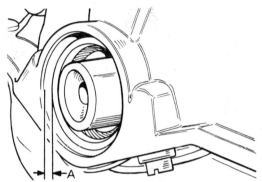

FIG 1:14 Install the timing case seal so that dimension A is 6.1mm (0.24in)

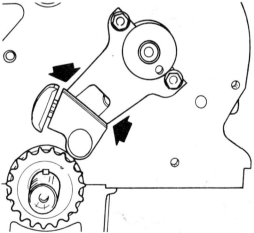

FIG 1:15 The camshaft thrust plate legs must be correctly located on assembly

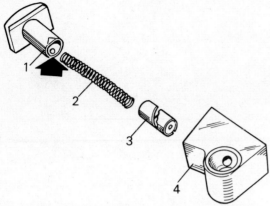

FIG 1:16   Timing chain tensioner components

Key to Fig 1:16   1 Sleeve and pad   2 Spring   3 Piston
4 Body

followed by the other two bearings in turn. The expansion
plug sealing the rear bearing is driven out with it.

To install the new bearings, start at the rear and work
towards the front of the crankcase. Locate each bearing
so that the notch is facing away from the crankshaft and
towards the front, as shown in **FIG 1:12**. This ensures
that the oilways line up with those in the crankcase. The
centre bearing has two oil holes, the smaller one lining up
with an oil feed to the rocker gallery, as shown in
FIG 1:13.

Make sure that the front bearing does not project
beyond the crankcase front face. Remove any over-
lapping bearing metal obstructing the oilways in the
crankcase. Fit a new expansion plug behind the rear
bearing, ensuring that there are no burrs or flats on the
rim of the plug. Use jointing compound to ensure an oil-
tight joint.

To renew the timing case oil seal, drive out the old seal
taking care not to damage the front bore of the case.
Drive the new seal in open side first, until the front face of

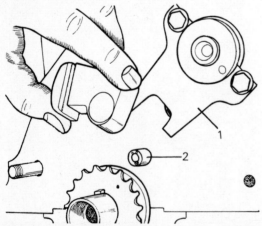

**FIG 1:17   Fitting the loaded chain tensioner, showing
the thrust plate 1 and oil nozzle 2**

the seal is 6.1mm (0.24in) below the face of the timing
case, as shown by dimension A in **FIG 1:14**. The use of
special tool VR2092 will facilitate installation of the seal.
Smear the lip of the seal with engine oil before installing
the crankshaft pulley. Note that this seal can be renewed
without the need for engine removal, after removing the
front anti-roll bar and the crankshaft pulley. In this case,
the old seal is removed by driving in one side of the seal
to tilt it in the bore then pulling it out with a piece of
hooked wire.

Lubricate and refit the tappets. Ensure that each tappet
is at the limit of its travel in order that it clears its cam.
Smear the cams and tappet faces with graphited oil and
carefully insert the camshaft. Refit the camshaft thrust
plate with the legs positioned as shown in **FIG 1:15**.
Check camshaft end float at the thrust plate. This should
be 0.05 to 0.23mm (0.002 to 0.009in). Excessive end
float must be cured by fitting a new thrust plate.

Timing chain tensioner components are shown in
FIG 1:16. When reassembling the tensioner, first install
the spring 2 and piston 3 in the sleeve 1. Engage the pip
in the sleeve with the piston groove. Press the tensioner
together, turning clockwise, until the pip engages in the
recess at the end of the piston groove. This will retain
the piston in the loaded state. Fit the assembly to
the tensioner body.

Excessive timing chain wear may indicate that the oil
nozzle, shown at 2 in **FIG 1:17**, is blocked or defective.
The nozzle is an interference fit in the crankcase. If a new
nozzle is fitted, note that the radial position of the oil hole
is not important.

Fit the tensioner assembly to the nozzle as shown in
FIG 1:17, noting that the tensioner must remain in its
loaded state during assembly otherwise it will be impossible to fit the sprockets and chain assembly.

Lubricate the timing chain with engine oil and assemble
the two sprockets with the chain so that the timing marks
align as shown at 2 in **FIG 1:18**. Make sure that the dowel
1 is in position. If the tensioner is released during this
operation, it will have to be removed and reset in the
loaded state before the chain can be installed.

Lubricate the timing case oil seal with engine oil, then
attach a new timing case gasket to the crankcase with
grease. Fit the timing case, making sure that the tensioner
pad lines up with the chain. Before tightening the timing
case bolts the oil seal must be concentric with the crankshaft. A special tool is available for this purpose. Tighten
the bolts alternatively and evenly to avoid distortion.
Refit the crankshaft pulley and bolt, then refit the oil pump
and sump as described later.

1:8 Removing sump and oil pump

The sump can be removed without the need for engine
removal, but the engine must be lifted to provide clearance
as follows:

Drain the cooling system and disconnect the radiator
hoses. Disconnect the steering gear coupling. Remove
four bolts securing the steering gear to the front crossmember and remove the front engine mounting nuts.
Drain the oil from the sump, then remove the bolts
securing the sump to the engine. Disconnect the gearbox
brace from the bottom of the sump. Note that, to maintain
frictional tension between the transmission brace 1 and

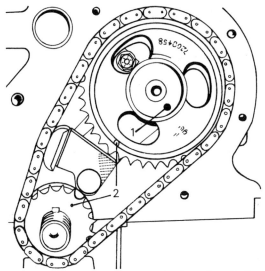

FIG 1:18 Timing chain and sprockets installation, showing alignment of dowel 1 and timing marks 2

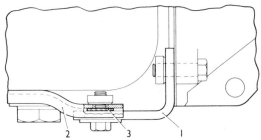

FIG 1:19 Transmission brace details, showing the lockwasher 3 which must be fitted between brace 1 and sump bracket 2

the sump bracket 2, an internal/external toothed lockwasher 3 must be fitted between the brace and bracket, as shown in **FIG 1:19**. Make sure that a washer of this type is in position when reassembling.

Fit the lifting equipment and raise the engine assembly sufficiently to allow removal of the sump. Remove and discard the sump gasket and the seal in the groove of the rear main bearing cap.

To remove the oil pump, turn the crankshaft by means of the pulley bolt until the pointer on the pulley is aligned with the TDC pointer on the timing case, with the distributor rotor pointing towards the segment for No. I plug lead in the distributor cap. Do not turn the engine after this. Remove the distributor as described in **Chapter 3**. Refer to **FIG 1:20** and remove the pump suction pipe support bolt 1. Remove the two bolts 2 and detach the oil pump and gasket. The oil strainer is a push fit on the suction pipe and can be removed for cleaning.

1:9 Servicing the oil pump

The oil pump components are shown in **FIG 1:21**. Pump efficiency depends on precise clearances between component parts. Overhaul does not call for special tools but involves accurate measurement of the various dimensions which will be found in **Technical Data**.

To dismantle the pump, remove the suction pipe from the pump cover. Remove the two remaining bolts in the cover and lift off the cover. Mark the meshed teeth of the impellers so that if the unit is serviceable they can be reassembled in the same mesh. Withdraw the driven impeller. Mark the position of the drive gear teeth in relation to the offset slot in the spindle. Unrivet the driving gear and withdraw the driving spindle and impeller assembly. Do not remove the impeller from the drive spindle unless these components are to be renewed. Check the components in the following manner, noting that if several parts need renewal it may be better to fit a replacement pump.

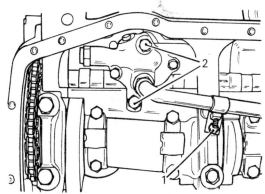

FIG 1:20 The suction pipe retaining bolt 1 and oil pump mounting bolts 2

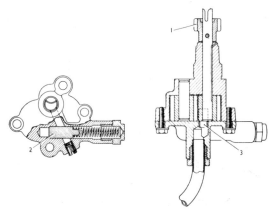

FIG 1:21 Sectional views of the oil pump, showing skew gear 1, pressure relief valve 2, and the pipe 3 which prevents oil drainage in service

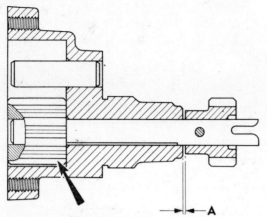

FIG 1:22 When installing a new pump drive gear (arrowed), end float A must be set as described in the text

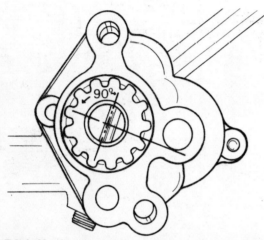

FIG 1:23 Correct position of drive spindle slot before oil pump installation. On later engines the slot is not offset

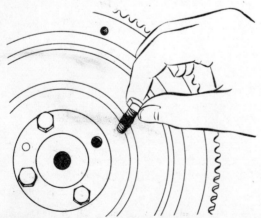

FIG 1:24 Special sealer must be applied to the centre part of each flywheel bolt before installation

Check both impellers for end clearance, radial clearance in the body and backlash between the teeth, using feeler gauges. Note that a worn driven impeller spindle or drive impeller spindle bore call for renewal of pump body and impeller assembly. If either the driven gear, driving spindle or drive impeller is worn, all three parts must be renewed. Check that the drive impeller is a tight fit on its spindle.

If the attaching face of the pump cover shows signs of wear it should be renewed complete with oil strainer pipe.

The oil pressure relief valve plunger must slide freely in the bottom cover but without slackness. Renew the spring if its condition is doubtful.

Make sure that all internal oilways are clear and thoroughly clean all parts before reassembly. After a final wash in petrol the parts must not be touched with rag, as the smallest piece of fluff could block an oilway.

Lubricate the spindles with special graphited oil. The driving impeller must be pressed onto its spindle so that when the impeller, arrowed in FIG 1:22 is in contact with the pump body, the end float measured at A is 0.18 to 0.25mm (0.007 to 0.010in). Refit the relief valve, then refit the sealing plug without using any sealing compound.

Before refitting the pump, check again that the pointer on the crankshaft pulley is aligned with the TDC mark on the timing case, with No. 1 piston on the compression stroke (both valves closed). To ensure that the pump spindle offset slot will be in the correct position when the pump is installed, turn the drive gear until the drive spindle slot is positioned as shown in FIG 1:23. On later engines the slot is on the spindle centre line to suit a modified distributor (see Chapter 3).

1:10 Removing clutch and flywheel

Remove the clutch from the flywheel in the manner described in Chapter 5. To remove the flywheel, unscrew the four bolts holding it to the crankshaft flange. Supporting the weight of the flywheel and keeping it square, tap it off the flange with a soft-faced hammer. If the flywheel is not kept square it may tend to jam on the shaft.

Check the clutch pilot bearing in the flywheel as described in Chapter 5.

Inspect the crankshaft key or dowel for wear or slackness and check the bolt holes for elongation due to the flywheel running loose. Examine the bolts for signs of stretching or damaged threads. If the flywheel has been running loose, remove any embedded metal from the crankshaft flange with carborundum taking care to protect the pilot bearing and the crankshaft oil seal from abrasive.

The starter ring gear should be renewed if it is badly worn or if broken teeth are found. The ring gear is shrunk onto the flywheel and renewal is a specialist job, so the work should be carried out by a fully equipped service station.

Before installing the flywheel bolts, apply Bostik 771 sealer to the centre part of each bolt as shown in FIG 1:24. Note that an excessive amount or an incorrect type of sealer may result in sealer exuding from the forward end of the bolt hole and contaminating the crankshaft oil seal. Tighten the bolts evenly and diagonally to a final torque of 30lb ft.

1:11 Connecting rods and bearings

For removal of connecting rods and pistons, the cylinder head and sump must be removed as described previously.

FIG 1:25 shows a piston and connecting rod assembly. Before dismantling the big-ends, mark each piston and connecting rod assembly and its cap with the cylinder number, using paint. Do not use a file or punch as such marks can lead to fatigue failure. The numbers or symbols which may be found on the rods and caps indicate matching parts but not the cylinder numbers. The piston crown has a notch which must face towards the front. The low compression pistons fitted to models for certain markets are identified by a letter L stamped on the piston crown.

Unscrew the big-end bolts and remove the caps and bearings. Keep all parts in the correct order for reassembling in their original positions. Remove the carbon from the top of each bore and withdraw the pistons and connecting rods through the top of the cylinder block.

If there has been a big-end bearing failure, the crankpin must be examined for damage and for transfer of metal to its surface. The oilway in the crankshaft must be checked to ensure that there is no obstruction. Big-end bearing clearance can be checked by the use of Plastigage, which is the trade name for a precisely calibrated plastic filament. The filament is laid along the bearing to be measured for working clearance, the bearing cap fitted and the bolts tightened to the specified torque. The bearing is then dismantled and the width of the flattened filament is measured with the scale supplied with the material. The bearing clearance can then be read off the scale.

Requirements for the use of Plastigage:

1 Each bearing must be measured separately and none of the remaining caps must be fitted when main bearings are checked.

2 Bearing surfaces must be clean and free from oil, and the plastic strip must be laid along the bearing from front to rear.

3 The crankshaft must not be turned during measuring procedures.

4 The point at which the measurement is taken must be close to the respective dead centre position.

5 No hammer blows must be applied to the bearing or cap.

Procedure:

Place a length of plastic filament identical to the width of the bearing on the journal and fit the main or big-end bearing cap with shells and tighten to the specified torque. Remove the bearing cap and measure the width of the flattened filament to obtain the running clearance of the bearing. Check the figure with that given in **Technical Data**. If the bearing running clearance is too high, new bearing shells must be selected by the measurement procedures to bring the running clearance to within the specified limits.

If the big-end bearing journals or crankshaft main bearing journals are worn below the limits or are damaged in any way, the journals or bearings must be reground to accept suitable undersize bearing shells, this being a specialist job.

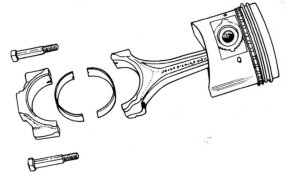

FIG 1:25 Piston and connecting rod assembly

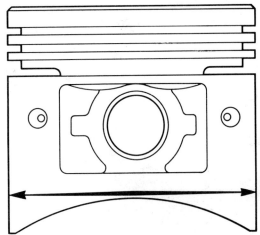

FIG 1:26 Piston diameter must be measured at right angles to the gudgeon pin bore and 9mm (0.36in) from the bottom of the skirt

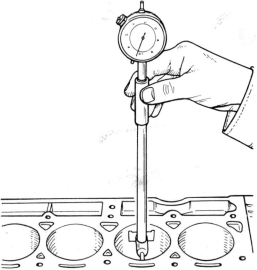

FIG 1:27 Checking the inside diameter of cylinder bores

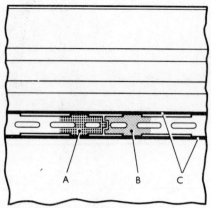

FIG 1:28 The correct assembly of oil scraper rings to the piston is described in the text

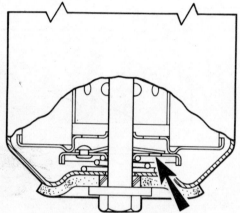

FIG 1:29 Oil filter bypass holes

1:12 Pistons, rings and gudgeon pins

Clean carbon deposits from the piston crowns, then gently ease the rings from their grooves and remove them over the tops of the pistons. Keep all rings in the correct order for refitting in their original positions, if they are not to be renewed. Clean carbon from the piston ring grooves, for which job a piece broken from an old piston ring and ground to a chisel point will prove an ideal tool. Inspect the pistons for score marks or any signs of seizure, which would dictate renewal.

Fit the piston rings one at a time into the bore from which they were removed, pushing them down with the inverted piston to ensure squareness. Measure the gap between the ends of the ring when it is positioned in the bore, using feeler gauges. Remove the ring from the bore and hold it in the piston groove from which it was removed, then measure the side clearance with feeler gauges. Compare the measurements taken with the figures given in **Technical Data**. If the clearance measurement in either test is at or near the wear limit, new rings must be fitted. Excessive ring clearance can be responsible for high oil consumption and poor engine performance.

Check the cylinder bores for score marks and remove glaze and carbon deposits. Badly scored or worn surfaces will dictate a rebore to accept new pistons, this being a specialist job. The fitting of new pistons to connecting rods must be carried out by a fully equipped service station, due to the need for special tools and press equipment to remove and refit the gudgeon pin.

Check the clearance of each piston in its bore. To do this, measure the outside diameter of the piston and the inside diameter of the bore and compare the two figures. The clearance limits are given in **Technical Data**. As the piston skirt is ground both oval and tapered, it is essential that piston size is measured only at right angles to the gudgeon pin and 9mm (0.36in) from the bottom of the skirt, as shown in **FIG 1:26**. The micrometer spindle must turn freely so that it can be adjusted to the piston with a very light turning effort. If the micrometer is adjusted too tightly against the piston, it will indicate a dimension significantly smaller than the actual size. For maximum accuracy in checking cylinder bores, it is essential to use a cylinder gauge in conjunction with the same micrometer as used for measuring the piston, as shown in **FIG 1:27**. This avoids any discrepancy between individual micrometers. Excessive clearance will dictate the fitting of new pistons and rings and, possibly, reboring of the cylinders. This is a specialist job.

When refitting the rings to the pistons, scraper ring spacers must be assembled to the piston bottom grooves so that ends A and B do not overlap, but have their ends engaged as shown in **FIG 1:28**. The ends of rails C and spacer should be positioned equally around the piston. Install the second ring with the stepped face to the bottom of the piston. The top ring, which is barrel shaped and chrome plated, can be installed either way up. Space all ring gaps evenly around the piston.

1:13 Removing crankshaft and main bearings

The crankshaft runs in three main bearings of the shell type. Crankshaft end float is controlled at the centre main bearing position, the upper shell being flanged and positively located in the crankcase.

To remove the crankshaft, the sump, flywheel and piston and connecting rod assemblies must first be removed as described in previous sections. Mark the main bearing caps with paint to ensure that they will be refitted in their original positions. Remove the main bearing bolts and caps, keeping each shell with its respective cap. Check that the crankshaft end float is between 0.05 and 0.20mm (0.002 and 0.008in). Lift out the crankshaft and discard the crankshaft oil seals. Remove the bearing shells from the crankcase, again keeping them in the correct order.

If there has been a main bearing failure, the crankshaft journal must be checked for damage and for transfer of metal to its surface. The oilways in the crankshaft must be checked to ensure that there is no obstruction. Main bearing clearance can be checked by the use of Plastigage, in the manner described in **Section 1:11** for big-end bearings, the procedure being the same. If there is any doubt about the condition of the crankshaft it should be taken to a specialist for more detailed checks.

1:14 External oil filter

The oil filter is of the fullflow type, having a renewable element and a bypass device which allows oil to pass directly from the pump to the engine if the filter should become blocked.

The filter is on the lefthand side of the crankcase. Before removal, place an oil tray beneath as some oil will escape even if the sump has been drained. Unscrew the centre bolt and remove the casing. Remove and discard the element. Remove the old seal from the seating in the block. In case of difficulty, pry out the seal with a sharply pointed instrument, but do not prise it out by levering against the edge of the groove. Clean out the filter casing and ensure that the bypass holes, arrowed in **FIG 1:29**, are clear.

Refit the filter casing with a new element and a new seal. Ensure that the casing seats on the seal and does not foul the edge of the groove, then tighten the bolt to a torque of 14lb ft. If the sump has been drained it should be refilled, otherwise top up to compensate for oil drained from the filter. Run the engine to check for leaks.

1:15 Reassembling stripped engine

Before starting this work, make sure that all components are clean. On a major overhaul the plugs in the cylinder block should be unscrewed from the main oil gallery and the gallery blown out with compressed air. Coat the threads with sealing compound when refitting the plugs. The water passages in the head should be flushed out with water. New gaskets and oil seals should be used throughout, and all moving parts should be lubricated with engine oil during assembly, except where otherwise indicated.

When refitting the crankshaft, ensure that the new rear oil seal is clean and undamaged. Check the periphery of the crankshaft flange, including the chamfer, for scores, burrs or scratches which can damage the seal. Lubricate the oil seal lip and the crankshaft flange with anti-scuffing paste. Fit the seal squarely on the flange, taking care that the seal lip which faces towards the main bearing is not turned back or damaged. Ensure that all traces of old jointing compound have been removed from the oil seal groove and rear main bearing cap faces on the crankcase and remove all traces of oil from these surfaces with solvent. After drying apply jointing compound sparingly to the oil seal grooves. Install the crankcase halves of the main bearing shells. The flanged shell is for the centre bearing. This shell should be renewed if crankshaft end float was outside limits as described previously. Lubricate the shells with engine oil.

Carefully lower the crankshaft into position, taking the weight while guiding the oil seal into its groove in the crankcase, as shown in **FIG 1:30**. On no account must the weight of the crankshaft rest on the seal lip or the seal will be permanently damaged. Recheck the crankshaft end float as described previously.

Install the main bearing caps with their shells. The centre cap has the tapped hole for the oil suction pipe bolt on the side nearest the camshaft.

The rear main bearing cap must be fitted correctly, in the following manner.

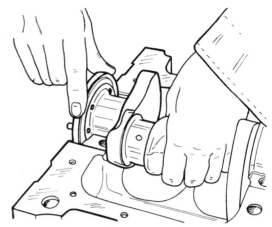

FIG 1:30 Supporting the weight of the crankshaft while installing the rear oil seal

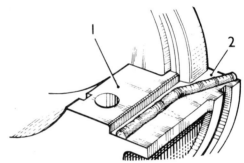

FIG 1:31 Application of sealer to register of rear main bearing cap

Use suitable solvent to remove all traces of jointing compound and oil, then dry the surfaces. Apply jointing compound sparingly to the inner seal groove of the cap. Apply Silastic 732 RTV sealant in a 3mm (0.12in) wide bead on cap register 2 far enough from the vertical face to prevent the sealant from being squeezed onto face I during installation of the cap, as shown in **FIG 1:31**. The sealant air hardens so the cap must be installed within five minutes of sealant application.

Fit the main bearing cap bolts with oiled threads and tighten to a torque of 82lb ft. It is essential for these bolts to be tightened to the specified torque.

Check that the piston rings are correctly fitted as described in **Section 1:12**. Lubricate the gudgeon pins with graphited oil and the cylinder bores, pistons and rings with clean engine oil. Using a suitable piston ring compressor, install each piston and rod assembly through the top of the cylinder bore, with the notch in the piston crown facing the front. When refitting original pistons, fit each into its original bore.

Make sure that the bearing shells are properly fitted in the connecting rods. Assemble the big-end caps and shells in their original order, aligning the paint marks made previously. Smear the bearing shells with engine

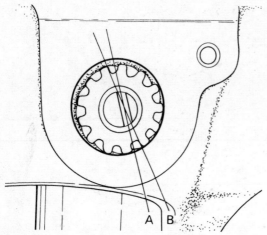

FIG 1:32 Checking the installed position of the oil pump drive spindle. On later models the slot is not offset

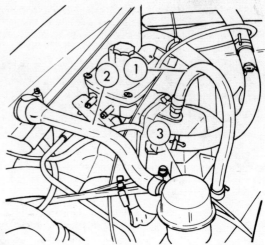

FIG 1:35 Crankcase ventilation from engine number 1817784

Key to Fig 1:35   1 Hose from rocker cover to intake manifold   2 Hose connection between breather and air cleaner   3 Combined breather and oil filter cap

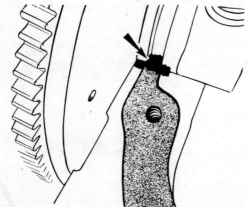

FIG 1:33 Sealer applied to gasket end and seal groove when fitting sump gasket

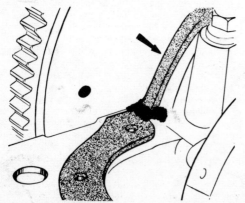

FIG 1:34 Ends of seal (arrowed) overlap gasket equally on each side. Apply sealer as shown

oil. Install the big-end bolts with oiled threads and tighten to a torque of 25lb ft. It is essential for these bolts to be tightened to the specified torque.

Refit the timing gear and oil pump as described previously. After the oil pump has been refitted, check that the driving spindle slot has taken up the position shown in **FIG 1:32**, or within 12° anticlockwise of that position, within the range A to B. If incorrect, remove the pump and reposition the drive spindle as described previously. Install the suction pipe and strainer, checking that the nut of the support screw is adjacent to the support attachment bolt. The following instructions must be carefully followed when refitting the sump, or leakage may result:

Inspect the sump contact faces for damage or distortion, then clean all old jointing compound from the sump and crankcase faces. Clean sealer from the rear main bearing cap groove unless this has recently been installed in which case, if the sealer has not hardened, it should not be removed. Dry the cleaned areas.

Apply jointing compound to the sump gasket area of the crankcase and timing case. Apply Silastic 732 RTV sealer to the corners formed by the rear bearing cap seal groove and the crankcase. Fit the new sump gasket onto the crankcase, making sure that the ends are fully engaged in the rear main bearing cap groove, then apply Silastic 732 RTV sealer as shown by the arrow in **FIG 1:33**.

Warm the bearing seal and shape into the contour of the bearing cap with the chamfered portion facing inwards. Fit the seal, arrowed in **FIG 1:34**, in the cap groove, ensuring that it overlaps the sump gasket equally at each side. Apply Silastic 732 RTV sealer to the junction of seal and gasket on both sides.

Jointing compound is not used between the gasket and the sump face and both these surfaces should be clean and dry. Install the sump within five minutes of sealant application, to avoid the possibility of the sealant hardening, making sure that the seal remains correctly seated in its groove. Tighten the sump bolts alternately and evenly.

If the bolts securing the front engine mounting brackets to the crankcase have been disturbed, degrease the bolt threads and the internal threads in the crankcase with solvent. Refit the bolts after smearing the threads with Loctite Grade AVV to ensure an oil and watertight seal and prevent the bolts from working loose.

Refit the flywheel as described previously and the clutch as described in **Chapter 5**.

1:16 Refitting the engine

Refit any further items removed from the engine after removal from the car. Apply a light smear of grease to the splines of the gearbox input shaft and ensure that the clutch release lever and bearing are correctly positioned (see **Chapter 5**).

Lower the engine into position, lining it up very carefully so that the gearbox input shaft enters the splined clutch hub and crankshaft spigot bearing. It is essential to avoid allowing the weight of the engine to hang on the splined shaft, otherwise considerable damage may be caused.

Refit all remaining components in the reverse order of removal. Refill the sump with the recommended grade of engine oil and refill the cooling system. Start the engine and run it until normal working temperature is reached, then check the carburetter settings and examine the engine for leaks. Check the tightness of cylinder head bolts and the valve clearances, as described previously.

1:17 Fault diagnosis

(a) Engine will not start

1 Defective coil
2 Faulty distributor capacitor
3 Dirty, pitted or incorrectly set contact points
4 Ignition leads loose or insulation faulty
5 Water on plug leads
6 Battery discharged or terminals corroded
7 Faulty or jammed starter
8 Sparking plug leads wrongly connected
9 Vapour lock in fuel pipes
10 Defective fuel pump
11 Over choking or 'pumping' accelerator pedal
12 Under choking
13 Blocked fuel filter or carburetter jets
14 Leaking valves
15 Sticking valves
16 Valve timing incorrect
17 Ignition timing incorrect

(b) Engine stops

1 Check 1, 2, 3, 4, 10, 11, 12, 13, 14, 15 in (a)
2 Retarded ignition
3 Weak mixture
4 Water in fuel system
5 Fuel tank vent blocked
6 Incorrect valve clearances

(c) Engine idles badly

1 Check 2 and 6 in (b)
2 Air leak at manifold joints
3 Slow running jet blocked or out of adjustment
4 Air leak in carburetter
5 Over rich mixture
6 Worn piston rings
7 Worn valve stems or stem bores
8 Weak valve springs

(d) Engine misfires

1 Check 1, 2, 3, 4, 5, 8, 10, 13, 14, 15, 16, 17 in (a); 2, 3, 4, 6 in (b)
2 Weak or broken valve springs

(e) Engine overheats (see **Chapter 4**)

(f) Compression low

1 Check 14, 15 in (a); 7, 8 in (c); 2 in (d)
2 Worn piston ring grooves
3 Scored or worn cylinder bores

(g) Engine lacks power

1 Check 3, 10, 11, 13, 14, 15, 16, 17 in (a); 2, 3, 4, 6 in (b); 7, 8 in (c); 2 in (d); also check (e) and (f)
2 Leaking joint washers or gaskets
3 Fouled sparking plugs
4 Automatic advance not working

(h) Burnt valves or seats

1 Check 14, 15 in (a); 6 in (b); 2 in (d). Also check (e)
2 Excessive carbon around valve seat and head

(j) Sticking valves

1 Check 2 in (d)
2 Bent valve stems
3 Scored valve stems
4 Incorrect valve clearance

(k) Excessive cylinder wear

1 Check 11 in (a)
2 Lack of oil
3 Dirty oil
4 Piston rings gummed or broken
5 Badly fitting piston rings
6 Connecting rod bent

(l) Excessive oil consumption

1 Check 6, 7 in (c) and check (k)
2 Ring gaps too wide
3 Oil return holes in piston blocked
4 Scored cylinders
5 Oil level too high
6 External oil leaks

(m) Crankshaft and connecting rod bearing failure

1 Check 2 in (k)
2 Restricted oilways
3 Worn journals or crankpins
4 Loose bearing caps
5 Extremely low oil pressure
6 Damaged or faulty connecting rod

(n) Internal water leakage (see **Chapter 4**)

(o) **Poor circulation** (see **Chapter 4**)

(p) **Corrosion** (see **Chapter 4**)

(q) **High fuel consumption** (see **Chapter 2**)

(r) **Engine vibration**

1 Loose alternator bolts
2 Fan blades out of balance
3 Faulty or loose engine mountings
4 Exhaust pipe mountings too tight

CHAPTER 2

THE FUEL SYSTEM

2:1 Description

Fuel from the rear mounted tank is supplied to the carburetter by a mechanical type fuel pump operated from a special eccentric on the engine camshaft.

A Zenith Stromberg 150 CD-SEV carburetter is fitted, which operates on a constant vacuum principle and incorporates a single variable jet controlled by a plunger type air valve and metering needle. A disc type cold start device on the carburetter is manually operated by means of the choke control on the dashboard.

A paper element type air cleaner unit is fitted, the air intake being fitted with a vacuum motor which operates a control damper assembly. This regulates the temperature of the air entering the cleaner by opening and closing hot air and cold air ports in the intake tube.

2:2 Routine maintenance

At the intervals recommended in the owner's handbook the air cleaner element should be renewed and the fuel pump filter removed and cleaned.

The fuel tank vent pipe must be checked occasionally to ensure that it is clear, as the pump cannot function correctly unless there is atmospheric pressure on the fuel in the tank. The tank vent pipe is supported behind the body inner side panel by a clip, the pipe outlet protruding through the rear compartment floor.

The oil level in the carburetter damper should be checked periodically, as described in **Section 2:6**.

2:3 Air cleaner

The air cleaner system, shown in **FIG 2:1**, incorporates temperature sensing unit 1, a vacuum motor 2 and a hot air shroud 3. The vacuum motor operates the control damper assembly which regulates the temperature of intake air. Hot air is drawn from a shroud covering the exhaust manifold and is directed to the air intake through a flexible hose. Cold air is drawn in through the main intake pipe. Under most operating conditions, both ports will be partially open, the extent of opening of each port being automatically adjusted to control intake temperature as required.

When the engine is running, the amount of vacuum in the motor depends on the temperature sensor unit in the air cleaner which is located in the vacuum line between inlet manifold and vacuum motor. The sensor unit incorporates a bi-metal temperature sensing spring which starts to open a valve to bleed more air into the vacuum line whenever the temperature in the air cleaner rises

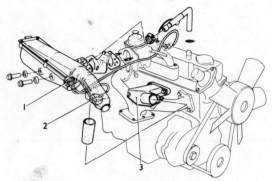

FIG 2:1 Air cleaner mounting details

Key to Fig 2:1   1 Temperature sensing unit   2 Vacuum motor   3 Hot air shroud

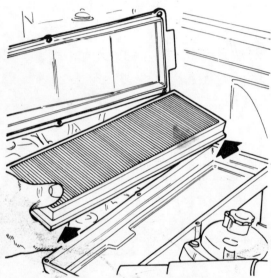

FIG 2:2 Air filter element renewal. The sealing ring (arrowed) must be towards the air cleaner body

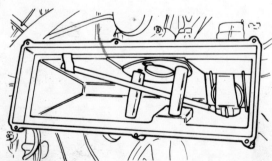

FIG 2:3 Using a thermometer to check air cleaner sensor unit

above 40°C. When the temperature falls below this figure, the spring begins to close the air bleed into the vacuum line thereby allowing more manifold vacuum to reach the vacuum motor.

When starting a cold engine, with air cleaner temperature below 33°C, the cold air port will be closed and the hot air port will open immediately. The cold air port will remain tightly closed for only a few minutes. As soon as hot air from the exhaust manifold is received by the air cleaner unit, the sensor will cause the damper to move and partially uncover the cold air port, mixing cold and hot air as necessary to regulate air cleaner temperature to within plus or minus 7°C of the ideal 40°C air intake temperature. Accelerating the engine hard will cause the vacuum level in the inlet manifold and vacuum motor to drop. When vacuum drops sufficiently, the diaphragm spring will move the damper so that the cold air port is fully open. This allows maximum airflow for acceleration.

A fault in the sensor unit or vacuum motor will generally result in the damper closing the hot air port and keeping the cold air port open. In warm or hot weather, the fault will probably go unnoticed. However, in cold weather this fault may result in hesitation or stalling of the engine, due to an excessively lean mixture. Checks for the vacuum motor and sensor operation are given later in this section.

Renewing filter element:

Remove the six screws, detach the air cleaner cover and lift out the element as shown in **FIG 2:2**. Discard the old filter element. Wipe clean the inside of the casing and cover, then fit a new element in the reverse order of removal. The rubber sealing ring on the element (arrowed) must face towards the air cleaner body.

Checking vacuum motor:

First make a check on all hoses for correct routing. Check for kinked, blocked or damaged hoses. Switch off the engine and use a mirror to observe the position of the damper through the air cleaner intake. The cold air port should be open and the hot air port closed. If damper position is incorrect, check the linkage for binding.

To check the operation of the motor diaphragm, a vacuum pump will be needed. Detach the hose from the vacuum motor and attach the pipe from the vacuum pump. Apply at least 0.27 bar (9in Hg) of vacuum to the motor diaphragm. When this is done, the damper should close the cold air port and open the hot air port. If not, check that the linkage is connected correctly and that there are no vacuum leaks. With the vacuum still applied, bend or clamp the hose to trap the vacuum in the motor unit. The damper should remain with the cold air port closed and hot air port open. If not, there is a vacuum leak in the diaphragm unit and the vacuum motor and intake tube assembly must be renewed.

Checking sensor unit:

Check the position of the damper through the air cleaner intake as described previously. The cold air port should be fully open and the hot air port closed. Allow the engine to cool, so that the air cleaner is below a temperature of 33°C, before continuing with tests. Start the engine and allow it to idle. Immediately after starting the engine, the cold air port should be closed and the hot air port open. As the engine warms up, the damper should move to partially open the cold air port and the air cleaner should become warm to the hand.

If the system does not operate correctly, switch off the engine and allow it to cool down. Remove the air filter element as described previously, then fit a thermometer with its bulb adjacent to the sensor unit, retaining it with adhesive tape as shown in **FIG 2:3**. Refit the air cleaner cover. Start the engine and check that the air port closes immediately. When the engine has been idling for a few minutes, the damper will open the cold air port. When this occurs, remove the cover and read the thermometer. A reading between 33° and 47°C should be obtained. If the damper does not begin to open the cold air port at the temperature stated, the sensor unit is defective and must be renewed. The sensor is secured into the air cleaner body by a metal clip. Pull off the vacuum pipes and lever off the retaining clip. Fit a new unit in the reverse order.

2:4 Fuel pump

The fuel pump is a sealed assembly which cannot be dismantled for overhaul, only the filter unit being accessible for cleaning as described later. If the pump is found to be defective, it must be renewed.

Testing:

Before testing the pump, ensure that the fuel tank vent system is not blocked. If it is suspected that fuel is not reaching the carburetter, disconnect the carburetter feed pipe and hold a suitable container under the end of the pipe. Turn the engine over a few times with the starter and watch for fuel squirting from the end of the pipe, which indicates that the pump is working. If so, check the float needle in the carburetter for possible sticking.

Reduced fuel flow can be caused by blocked fuel pipes or a clogged filter. If an obstructed pipeline appears to be the cause of the trouble, it may be cleared with compressed air. Disconnect the pipeline at the pump and carburetter. **Do not pass compressed air through the pump or the valves will be damaged.** If there is an obstruction between the pump and the tank, remove the tank filler cap before blowing the pipe through from the pump end.

If the pump delivers insufficient fuel, suspect an air leak between the pump and the tank, dirt under the pump valves or faulty valve seatings. If no fuel is delivered, a sticking valve or faulty pump diaphragm are likely causes. Faults of this type will dictate pump renewal.

Filter cleaning:

Remove the single screw and detach the pump cover, filter and gasket, as shown in **FIG 2:4**.

Wash the filter and the inside of the pump cover and sediment chamber with clean petrol, using a small brush to remove stubborn deposits. If the filter is damaged or will not clean up properly it should be renewed. On completion, refit the filter and cover using a new gasket. Ensure that the four pegs on the filter are towards the top cover.

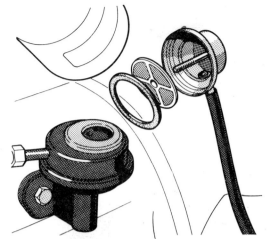
FIG 2:4 Fuel pump filter removal

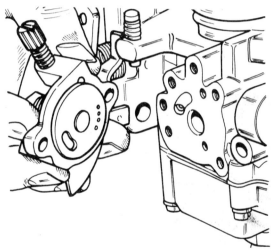
FIG 2:5 The cold start device removed from the carburetter

FIG 2:6 The carburetter temperature compensator, showing the blade 1 and plug 2. Item 3 is the idle trimming screw

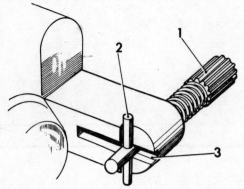

FIG 2:7 The spring-loaded stop for the cold start device

Key to Fig 2:7   1 Stop control   2 Pin   3 Groove

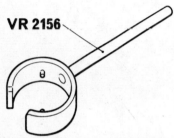

VR 2156

FIG 2:8 The special tool used to rotate the carburetter jet adjuster

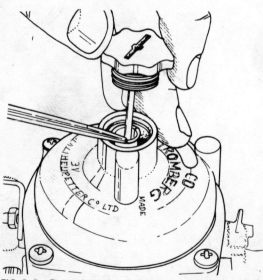

FIG 2:9 Removing the damper assembly to check damper oil level

Removing and refitting pump:

To remove the pump, disconnect the two hoses from the pump, plugging the inlet hose to prevent leakage. Undo the two bolts holding the pump to the crankcase and remove the pump and gasket.

Refit the pump in the reverse order of removal, making sure that the rocker arm contacts the eccentric on the camshaft correctly. Use a new gasket unless the original is in perfect condition. Tighten the fixing bolts alternately and evenly to avoid distortion of the mounting flange.

2:5 Carburetter operation

The Zenith Stromberg 150 CD-SEV carburetter is of the sidedraft pattern and operates on the constant vacuum principle with a variable jet controlled by a piston type air valve and metering needle. A separate enrichment assembly is fitted to provide the rich mixture required for cold starting, this component being shown in **FIG 2:5**. The disc is provided with a series of different diameter holes, these permitting fuel to pass from the float chamber into the mixing chamber when the choke control is operated, thus providing extra fuel to facilitate starting from cold.

To cater for minor mixture strength variations caused by heat transfer from the engine to carburetter body, a temperature compensator is provided as shown in **FIG 2:6**. This consists of a bi-metal blade 1 and a tapered plug 2 in a housing which is protected by a cover. Drillings in the body of the carburetter permit air from the front of the carburetter to bypass the air valve, this affecting the depression that controls the rise and fall of the air valve and needle assembly. The tapered plug controls the amount of air admitted through the bypass in response to the deflection of the bi-metal blade. The preset assembly requires no adjustment.

The choke control cable operates the fast-idle cam which is attached to the cold start device spindle. The cam contacts a screw on the throttle stop plate to open the throttle slightly and ensure a fast-idle when the engine is cold. A spring-loaded stop, shown in **FIG 2:7**, determines the movement of the fast-idle cam in the cold start position. In the position shown, the stop is set to provide correct enrichment for starting down to temperatures of −18°C. If ambient temperature is below this figure, the stop should be positioned so that the pin is engaged in groove 3 for maximum travel of the cold start device.

2:6 Slow-running adjustments

When the engine is new, a slightly weaker mixture is required and the idle trimming screw, shown at 3 in **FIG 2:6**, is initially set off its seat. If engine idling quality should deteriorate during the running-in period, rotate the screw clockwise until a smooth idle is obtained. If, when the screw is seated, idling is unsatisfactory, a check should be made on the inlet manifold and carburetter joint areas for air leakage. **Do not overtighten the idle trimming screw.**

Routine adjustment of the carburetter should be carried out after any ignition system or valve clearance adjustments or servicing have been carried out, or at any time if engine idle speed is incorrect. It must be pointed

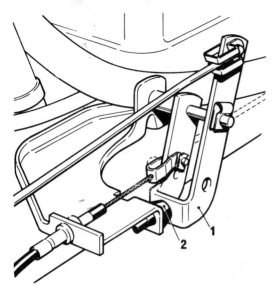

FIG 2:10   The throttle lever 1 and rubber stop 2

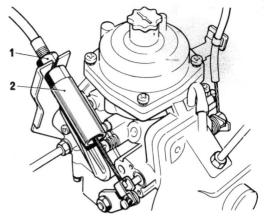

FIG 2:11   The throttle cable locknuts

out, however, that any carburetter adjustment will only be effective if the sparking plugs and ignition system are in good order and that the engine must be at normal operating temperature when they are carried out.

If the carburetter has been overhauled and the original settings lost, make an initial setting of the jet adjuster under the float chamber by unscrewing it two turns out from the fully in position. Use tool VR2156 or similar, as shown in **FIG 2:8**, to turn the jet adjuster.

Run the engine up to normal operating temperature, then remove the air cleaner assembly from the carburetter. Check that the oil level is correct in the carburetter hydraulic damper. This should be approximately 8mm (0.30in) below the top of the air valve guide. To check, remove the cap and damper assembly as shown in **FIG 2:9**. Insert a finger into the carburetter intake and lift the air valve, then top up the guide with 10W-30 engine oil. When installing the damper, raise the air valve and ensure that the cap is fully seated in the guide tube before screwing down.

Start the engine and allow it to idle. Adjust the throttle stop screw to obtain an engine idling speed of 800 to 850 rev/min. Now screw the jet adjuster in or out a little at a time until a smooth idle is obtained. Check the mixture setting by inserting a screwdriver between the carburetter bore and the underside of the air valve. Lift the air valve 1mm (0.04in), which should cause the engine speed to rise slightly momentarily then slow down. If the engine speed continues to rise, the mixture setting is too rich, so the jet adjuster should be screwed in a little at a time until the correct mixture strength is obtained. If the engine stalls when the air valve is lifted as described, the mixture is too weak, so the jet adjuster should be unscrewed a little at a time until the correct setting is obtained. On completion, refit the air cleaner assembly to the carburetter.

In territories where exhaust emission control regulations apply, the percentage of carbon monoxide (CO) in the exhaust gases at idling speed should be 2.5 to

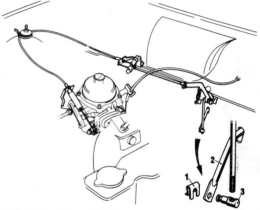

FIG 2:12   Throttle linkage components on lefthand drive vehicles

Key to Fig 2:12   1 Clip   2 Pedal lever   3 Swivel

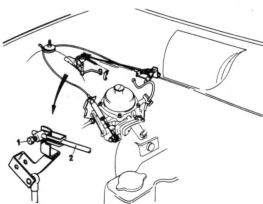

FIG 2:13   Throttle linkage components on righthand drive vehicles

Key to Fig 2:13   1 Clamp bolt   2 Rod

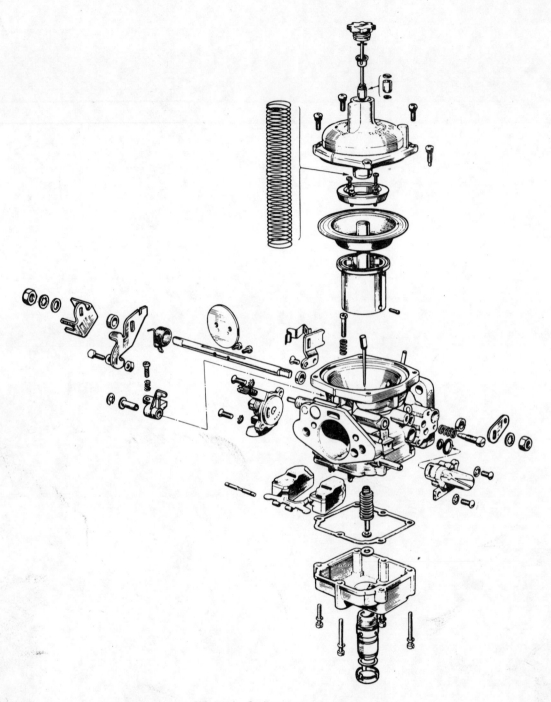

FIG 2:14   Carburetter components

3.5 per cent when the engine is at normal operating temperature. Special exhaust gas analysing equipment is required to check these settings. If such equipment is not available, checks should be made at a service station to make sure that CO emissions conform to legal requirements. The idle speed trimming screw is adjusted to obtain the necessary CO percentage, but the screw must not be rotated more than four turns off its seat.

2:7 Carburetter servicing

Removal and refitting:

Remove the air cleaner assembly from the carburetter. Disconnect the throttle and choke control mechanisms, the fuel inlet pipe and the vacuum advance pipe from the carburetter. Unscrew the retaining nuts and detach the carburetter and gasket from the inlet manifold flange.

Refit the carburetter in the reverse order of removal, using a new gasket. On completion, check the throttle cable and linkage adjustment as follows.

Throttle cable adjustment:

Refer to **FIG 2:10**. Disconnect one end of the linkage rod between the pedal and cable relay levers. Position the lever 1 against rubber stop 2 on the relay lever bracket. Hold the carburetter throttle lever in the closed position and rotate the cable locknuts 1 and 2, shown in **FIG 2:11**, to remove all slack from the throttle cable. From this position, unscrew nut 1 by $1\frac{1}{2}$ turns and tighten nut 2 to lock in this position. This will set the cable with the correct amount of free play.

Throttle linkage adjustment:

During this adjustment procedure the carburetter throttle lever should be secured in the fully open position by suitable means.

For lefthand drive vehicles, refer to **FIG 2:12**. Detach clip 1 from swivel 3 and remove the swivel from the pedal lever 2. Push the accelerator pedal fully to the car floor, then raise it 5mm (0.20in) from the floor and hold it in this position by suitable means. Now rotate the swivel on the rod until the swivel aligns with the hole in the pedal levers and reassemble the linkage.

For righthand drive vehicles, refer to **FIG 2:13**. Slacken clamp bolt 1 from the swivel. Press the throttle pedal fully to the floor, then raise it 10mm (0.40in) from the floor and secure it in this position by suitable means. Now position rod 2 through the swivel and tighten the clamp bolt.

Servicing:

Dismantle the carburetter into the order shown in **FIG 2:14**, carefully noting the positions of the components and laying them out on a clean sheet of paper. Mark shafts, levers and valves so that they will be reassembled in the correct relative positions. Use the correct size of screwdriver when removing components to avoid damage.

Clean all parts in petrol or in approved carburetter cleaner, then examine them for wear or damage. Renew any faulty parts. Clean jets and passages thoroughly using compressed air, clean petrol and a small stiff brush. **Do not use cloth for cleaning purposes as small**

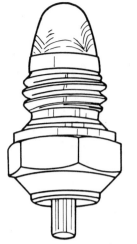

FIG 2:15 The needle valve and filter assembly

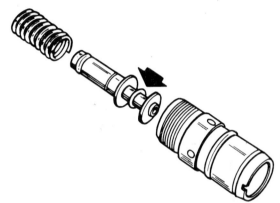

FIG 2:16 The nylon washer must be positioned between the flange and plain washer on the jet stem

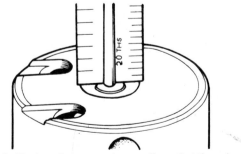

FIG 2:17 Install the metering needle so that the nylon washer is flush with the recessed face of the air valve

CHEVETTE

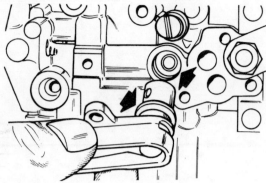

FIG 2:18 Temperature compensator installation, showing the positions of the rubber seals

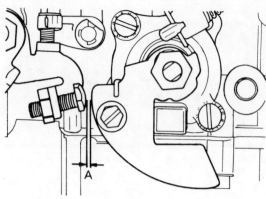

FIG 2:21 Correct clearance A between stop screw and fast idle cam is 2.5mm (0.10in)

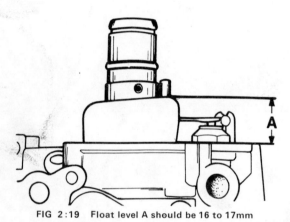

FIG 2:19 Float level A should be 16 to 17mm

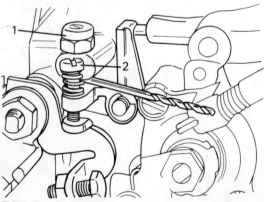

FIG 2:20 Float chamber ventilation valve adjustment

Key to Fig 2:20   1 Valve stop screw   2 Throttle stop screw

fibres may remain after cleaning and clog the jets or passages. Never use a wire probe as this will damage or enlarge the jets or passages.

Make sure that all sediment is cleared from the float chamber and inspect the float for damage or leakage, either of which will dictate renewal of the float assembly. Float leakage can usually be detected by shaking the float and listening for the sound of fuel splash inside.

The needle valve and filter assembly is shown in FIG 2:15. Clean the assembly thoroughly and inspect for wear or damage. Check that the valve is sealing correctly by blowing through from the filter end. The airflow should be cut off completely when the needle is held into the body by gentle finger pressure. Renew the assembly if there is any doubt about its condition. On completion, reassemble the carburetter in the reverse order of dismantling, noting the following points. Use new gaskets throughout and fit a new 'O' ring to the carburetter jet adjuster assembly.

When installing the jet assembly, make sure that the nylon washer is positioned on the jet stem between the flange and plain washer, as shown arrowed in FIG 2:16. The jet adjuster is sealed with a nylon plug which is installed in production after flow testing. No attempt should be made to remove the plug from the jet adjuster. Screw the jet adjuster fully into the carburetter body before installing the float chamber, otherwise the chamber may foul the adjuster shoulder before it seats on the carburetter body gaskets.

The metering needle is retained in the air valve by a single screw. Install the needle so that the nylon washer is flush with the recessed face of the air valve, as shown in FIG 2:17. The securing screw must coincide with the flat which is ground on the needle casing to ensure that the needle leans away from the depression holes in the valve face. Do not overtighten the needle securing screw. Fit the diaphragm to the air valve so that the lower tongue on the diaphragm is located in the slot provided in the valve. Install the valve and diaphragm so that the upper tongue on the diaphragm is located in the slot provided in the body.

When installing the temperature compensator, make sure that a rubber seal is fitted in the carburetter body and over the compensator post, as shown in FIG 2:18.

Before finally fitting the float chamber to the carburetter body, install the needle valve and float assembly and check for correct float level. To do this, invert the carburetter and allow the float assembly to rest on the needle valve, as shown in **FIG 2:19**. Dimension A, between the main body face and the highest point of each float should be 16 to 17mm. If the level is incorrect, adjust by carefully bending the tag which contacts the end of the needle.

When the carburetter is fully assembled, carry out the following adjustments:

Float chamber ventilation valve adjustment:

Refer to **FIG 2:20** and adjust stop screw 1 until a 2mm (No. 46) drill can be inserted between the valve lever and stop screw post as shown. Note that, if this adjustment is carried out in service, the position of throttle stop screw 2 may need to be adjusted to correct engine idling speed.

Fast-idle adjustment:

Refer to **FIG 2:21**. Slacken the locknut and adjust the stop screw until dimension A is 2.5mm (0.10in) between the screwhead and base of cam.

2:8 Fault diagnosis

(a) Leakage or insufficient fuel delivered

1 Air vent to tank restricted
2 Fuel pipe blocked
3 Air leaks at pipe connections
4 Fuel filter blocked
5 Pump gaskets faulty
6 Pump diaphragm defective
7 Pump valves sticking or seating badly

(b) Excessive fuel consumption

1 Carburetter requires adjustment
2 Fuel leakage
3 Sticking mixture control
4 Dirty air cleaner
5 Worn jets or passages in carburetter
6 Idling speed too high

(c) Idling speed too high

1 Incorrect adjustment
2 Throttle control sticking
3 Choke control sticking
4 Worn throttle valve assembly

(d) Noisy fuel pump

1 Loose pump mountings
2 Air leaks on suction side of pump
3 Obstruction in fuel pipeline
4 Clogged fuel filter

(e) No fuel delivery

1 Float needle valve stuck
2 Tank vent system blocked
3 Defective pump diaphragm
4 Pump valve stuck
5 Pipeline obstructed
6 Bad air leaks on suction side of pump

(f) Poor idling and loss of power

1 Carburetter diaphragm split
2 Metering needle sticking
3 Metering needle incorrect size
4 Throttle spindle worn

(g) Poor response to throttle

1 Oil level in damper low
2 Sticking air valve
3 Metering needle bent
4 Incorrect air valve spring fitted

NOTES

CHAPTER 3

THE IGNITION SYSTEM

3:1 Description

The ignition system is conventional, comprising an ignition coil, distributor and contact breaker assembly. The distributor incorporates automatic timing control by centrifugal mechanism and a vacuum operated unit. As engine speed increases, the centrifugal action of rotating weights pivoting against the tension of small springs moves the contact breaker cam relative to the distributor drive shaft and progressively advances the ignition. The vacuum control unit is connected by small bore pipe to a fitting on the carburetter. At high degrees of vacuum the unit advances the ignition, but under load, at reduced vacuum, the unit progressively retards the ignition.

The ignition coil is wound as an auto-transformer with the primary and secondary windings connected in series, the common junction being connected to the contact breaker with the positive feed from the battery going to the opposite terminal of the LT windings via the ignition switch. LT current supplied to the coil is via a resistance wire which reduces nominal battery voltage to approximately 6 volts at the coil terminal. This resistance wire is bypassed when the starter is in operation, so that full battery voltage is supplied to the coil. The coil then provides increased voltage to the HT system for maximum

sparking plug efficiency when the engine is being started.

When the contact breaker points are closed, current flows in the coil primary winding, magnetising the core and setting up a fairly strong magnetic field. Each time the contacts open, the battery current is cut off and the magnetic field collapses, inducing a high current in the primary winding and a high voltage in the secondary. The primary current is used to charge the capacitor connected across the contacts and the flow is high and virtually instantaneous. It is this high current peak which induces the surge in the secondary winding to produce the sparking voltage across the plug points. Without the capacitor the current peak would be much smaller and the sparking voltage considerably reduced, in fact to a point where it would be insufficient to fire the mixture in the engine cylinders. The capacitor, therefore, serves the dual purpose of minimising contact breaker wear and providing the necessary high charging surge to ensure a powerful spark.

3:2 Routine maintenance

Pull off the two spring clips and remove the distributor cap. Pull off the rotor arm to gain access to the contact

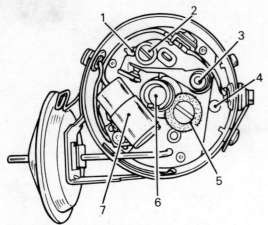

FIG 3:1 Distributor with cap and rotor removed

Key to Fig 3:1   1 Adjustment slot   2 Fixed contact screw
3 Moving contact pivot   4 Oil hole   5 Foam wick   6 Felt
pad   7 Capacitor

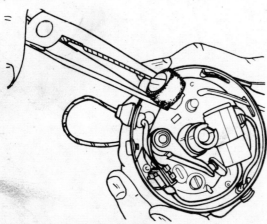

FIG 3:2 Removing the foam wick from the base plate

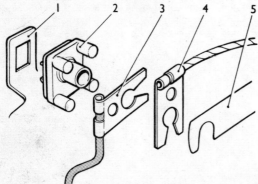

FIG 3:3 Contact breaker wiring and insulator assembly

Key to Fig 3:3   1 Fixed contact plate   2 Insulator
3 Capacitor terminal   4 LT terminal   5 Moving contact
spring

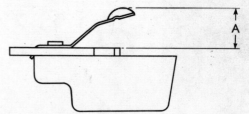

FIG 3:4 Dimension A must be 7.5 to 8.5mm (0.30 to
0.34in) to ensure correct rotor contact spring pressure

breaker points. Refer to **FIG 3:1** and apply a few drops of
engine oil through the hole 4 to lubricate the centrifugal
advance mechanism. Apply just enough oil to the felt pad
6 to soak it. Apply a single drop of oil to the pivot 3. The
foam wick 5 must be impregnated with lithium-based
grease, not oil. To remove the wick, squeeze together the
legs of the nylon support with a pair of long nosed pliers,
as shown in **FIG 3:2**. Apply grease sparingly to the wick
and work it well into the foam. If the wick is damaged or
contaminated with dirt, it should be discarded and a new
one fitted in its place. When lubricating the internal parts
of the distributor, take great care to avoid oil or grease
contaminating the contact breaker points, lubricating
sparingly for this reason.

Adjusting the contact breaker points:

Turn the engine until one of the cams has opened the
contact breaker points to their fullest extent, then check
the gap between the points with clean feeler gauges.
The correct gap is 0.50mm (0.020in). To adjust the gap,
loosen the fixed contact point clamp screw 2, insert a
screwdriver into slot 1, then turn the plate until the correct
gap is obtained (see **FIG 3:1**). Tighten the screw 2 and
recheck the gap. If new contact points have been
fitted, the gap should be set to 0.55mm (0.022in) to
allow for the initial bedding down of the new rubbing
block.

Cleaning the contact breaker points:

Use a fine carborundum stone or special contact
point file to polish the points if they are dirty or pitted,
taking care to keep the faces flat and square. If the points
are too worn to clean up in this manner, they should be
renewed. On completion of cleaning, wipe away all dust
with a cloth moistened in petrol.

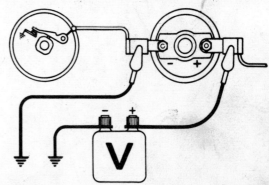

FIG 3:5 Voltmeter connections to test coil current
supply

Renewing the contact breaker points:

Refer to **FIG 3:3**. Use a small screwdriver to lever the moving contact spring 5 away from the insulator 2 then pull the moving contact from the pivot post. Detach the wiring connectors 3 and 4 and the insulator 2 from the fixed contact plate, then remove the fixing screw and lift the fixed contact from the base plate.

Wash the mating faces of the new contact points with methylated spirits to remove the protective coating. Fit the fixed contact point to the base plate and secure with the single screw. Fit the insulator and terminal connectors to the fixed contact plate, making sure that these parts are in the correct order as shown in **FIG 3:3**. Apply a drop of oil to the pivot post, then fit the moving contact and ease the spring into position. Set the contact points to the correct gap as described previously.

Checking rotor arm:

To ensure adequate rotor contact spring pressure, the dimension A shown in **FIG 3:4** must be 7.5 to 8.5mm (0.30 to 0.34in). Correct if necessary by carefully bending the spring blade. To check rotor insulation, remove the central HT lead from the distributor cap and hold it about $\frac{1}{2}$in from the edge of the rotor contact spring. To avoid shocks, hold the lead well away from the end. With the ignition switched on, flick open the contact points. If a spark jumps the gap the rotor is faulty and must be renewed.

3:3 Ignition faults

If the engine runs unevenly, set it to idle at approximately 1000 rev/min and, taking care not to touch any conducting part of the sparking plug leads, remove and replace each lead from its plug in turn. To avoid shocks during this operation it is necessary to wear a pair of thick gloves or to use insulated pliers. Doing this to a plug which is firing correctly will accentuate uneven running but will make no difference if the plug is not firing.

Having by this means located the faulty cylinder, stop the engine and remove the plug lead. Pull back the insulation or remove the connector so that the end of the lead is exposed. Alternatively, use an extension piece, such as a small bar or drill, pushed into the plug connector. Start the engine and hold the lead carefully to avoid shocks, so that the end is about $\frac{1}{8}$in away from the cylinder head. Crank the engine with the starter or flick open the contact points with the ignition switched on. A strong, regular spark confirms that the fault lies with the sparking plug which should be removed and cleaned as described in **Section 3:6**, or renewed if defective.

If the spark is weak and irregular, check the condition of the lead and, if it is perished or cracked, renew it and repeat the test. If no improvement results, check that the inside of the distributor cap is clean and dry and that there is no sign of tracking, which can be seen as a thin black line between the electrodes or between some metal part in contact with the cap. Tracking can only be cured by fitting a new cap. Check also that the contact in the centre of the rotor arm is set correctly, as shown in **FIG 3:4**. Check the contact button inside the cap for wear or damage, and the brass segments for wear or burning. Renew the cap if any fault is found.

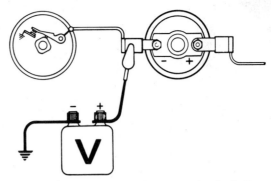

FIG 3:6 Voltmeter connections to check coil windings, contact breaker and capacitor

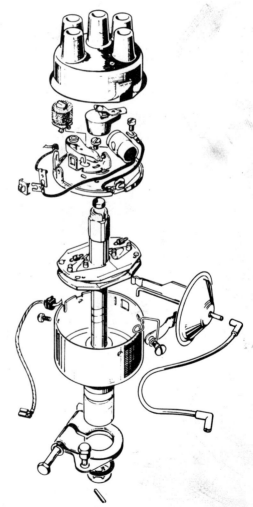

FIG 3:7 Distributor components

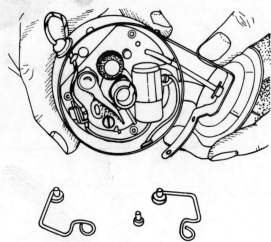

FIG 3:8 Removing the vacuum control unit from the distributor body

If these checks do not cure a weak HT spark, or if no spark can be obtained at the plug or lead, check the LT circuit as described next.

Testing the low tension circuit:

A 12-volt test lamp can be used to check circuit continuity, but accurate checking of the components requires the use of a voltmeter due to the differing voltages supplied to the coil during starting and running.

Checking coil current supply:

Connect the voltmeter positive to the coil positive terminal and the voltmeter negative to a good earth on the car engine or body, then connect a jumper lead from the coil negative to a good earth (see FIG 3:5).

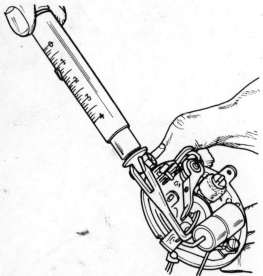

FIG 3:9 Checking the frictional resistance between upper and lower contact breaker plates

To check the starting supply to the coil, turn the ignition key to the start position and crank the engine. While the engine is turning on the starter, the voltmeter should register at least 8 volts. A low or zero reading may be due to faulty contacts in the starter solenoid switch or to defective wiring. To check the running supply to the coil through the resistance wire, switch on the ignition without starting the engine, when the voltmeter should register 4.5 to 6 volts. A voltmeter reading outside the limits stated indicates a fault in the resistance wire. Note that this wire cannot be serviced separately from the wiring harness.

Primary winding, contact breaker and capacitor check:

This check involves turning the engine, which should be carried out using a spanner of the correct size on the crankshaft pulley mounting bolt. The engine will be easier to turn if all of the sparking plugs are removed first. Connect the voltmeter positive to the coil negative terminal, and the voltmeter negative to a good earth on the engine or body as shown in FIG 3:6.

Remove the distributor cap and position it to one side. Turn the engine until the contact points are open, then switch on the ignition. The voltmeter should register battery voltage (11.5 to 12 volts). If there is no reading, there is a break in the coil primary winding or there is a shortcircuit in either the contact breaker connection or in the capacitor.

Turn the engine until the contact breaker points are closed, then switch on the ignition. The voltmeter reading should be zero to .2 volt. If over .2 volt, the contact points are dirty, the contact breaker plate and/or distributor housing earth is faulty, or the white/black wire has a break in it.

3:4 Removing and dismantling distributor

Removal:

FIG 3:7 shows the distributor components. Remove the distributor cap and place it to one side, then disconnect the white/black lead at the coil and pull off the vacuum pipe which is attached to a fitting on the distributor vacuum unit.

To avoid disturbing the timing, do not slacken the horizontal bolt and nut in the distributor clamp, but remove the vertical screw securing the clamp to the crankcase. The distributor can then be withdrawn vertically. To avoid altering the timing settings, do not turn the engine while the distributor is removed.

Dismantling:

Remove the three screws and detach the vacuum control unit, as shown in FIG 3:8. The contact breaker plate assembly can then be withdrawn. Do not attempt to dismantle the contact breaker plate as this is serviced as a complete unit only. The contact breaker points and the foam wick lubricator can be renewed as described in Section 3:2.

The contact breaker upper plate must rotate smoothly. Use a spring balance attached to the fixed contact plate lug to check the frictional resistance between the upper and lower plates, as shown in FIG 3:9. The force required to rotate the upper plate should be between 10 and 16oz. If resistance is outside these limits, the entire assembly should be renewed.

If the distributor mainshaft is to be removed, support the shaft and drift out the retaining pin. Remove the tabbed and plain thrust washers, then withdraw the shaft from the body. Be sure to remove any burrs from the shaft which would damage the bearing bushes during shaft removal. Before refitting the shaft, lubricate the felts in the housing and cam with engine oil. Fit the upper thrust washer to the shaft, then insert the shaft into the housing and secure with the tabbed thrust washer 2 and new pin 1, as shown in **FIG 3 :10**. Use feeler gauges to check the shaft end float as shown. This should be between 0.05 and 0.13mm (0.002 and 0.005in). If not within limits, a new distributor shaft should be fitted. The retaining pin hole should be drilled in the new shaft using a No. 30 drill. This hole can be located in any radial position, but must be located axially so that, with the shaft and thrust washers installed, end float is within the limits stated. Complete reassembly of the distributor in the reverse order of dismantling.

Refitting :

If the distributor housing clamp bolt has not been slackened and the engine has not been turned since the distributor was removed, line up the distributor shaft tongue with the offset in the oil pump spindle and insert the distributor. Secure the clamp plate to the crankcase with the vertical fixing screw. Adjust the contact points as described in **Section 3 :2**, then fit the rotor and distributor cap. Reconnect the wire to the coil.

The removal and refitting method described ensures that the distributor shaft has been replaced in the same position relative to the engine crankshaft, but the fitting of new parts and the adjustment of contact points can affect the timing to some extent, so it is advisable to check the ignition timing as described in the next section.

3:5 Timing the ignition

If the distributor has been removed and the timing setting lost, remove the rocker cover and turn the engine forwards until both valves at No. 1 (front) cylinder are closed and the timing pointer on the crankshaft pulley is aligned with the fixed pointer as shown in **FIG 3 :11**. Now align the distributor shaft tongue with the offset in the oil pump spindle. Push the distributor body fully home, secure the clamp plate to the crankcase, then complete the timing procedure as described next.

Turn the engine in the normal direction of forward rotation until the pointer 1 on the crankshaft pulley is aligned with the fixed pointer 2 on the crankcase as shown in **FIG 3 :11**. This sets the engine to the correct timing point of 9° BTDC. Check that the contact breaker points are clean and correctly set as described in **Section 3 :2**. On later models the shaft tongue is on the centre line to suit a modified oil pump spindle. The process of timing the ignition is the same as for the offset spindle tongue, except that when the distributor is installed the rotor arm should be in the position shown in **FIG 3 :12**.

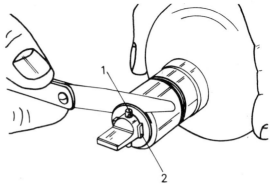

FIG 3 :10 Checking distributor shaft end float, showing retaining pin 1 and tabbed thrust washer 2

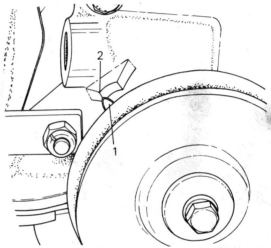

FIG 3 :11 Correct alignment of the engine timing marks

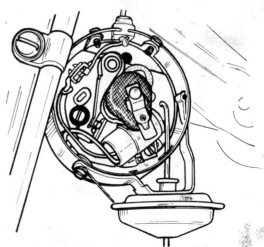

FIG 3 :12 Position of distributor rotor arm when timing the ignition

Connect a suitable test lamp in parallel with the contacts. One lead will go to the terminal on the side of the distributor and one to earth. Slacken the horizontal bolt and nut which secures the clamp to the distributor just sufficiently to allow the distributor body to be rotated by hand. Turn the distributor body anticlockwise as far as possible to ensure that the contact points are fully closed. Now switch on the ignition and turn the distributor body very slowly in a clockwise direction until the lamp just lights up. Without moving the distributor from this position, tighten the clamp bolt. This will correctly set the ignition timing.

Stroboscopic timing:

If this method of timing is used, the engine must be run until it reaches normal operating temperature then the vacuum line must be removed from the distributor and the end of the line plugged with a suitable screw or sealed by clamping. The normal idling speed should be reduced to approximately 600 rev/min to avoid faulty results due to the operation of the centrifugal advance mechanism. Connect the stroboscopic lamp equipment according to the manufacturer's instructions. Slacken the distributor clamp bolt, start the engine and allow it to idle slowly. Taking care to avoid the fan and drive belt, shine the lamp onto the timing marks and turn the distributor body until they appear in alignment as shown in **FIG 3 : 11**. Tighten the distributor clamp bolt, switch off the ignition and remove the stroboscopic timing equipment. Reconnect the vacuum line, then reset the engine idling speed to the normal level.

3:6 Sparking plugs

Sparking plugs should be of the recommended type, details of which are given in **Technical Data**. The gaps should be set to 1.0mm (0.040in) by bending the outer electrode only. Plugs can be cleaned and tested under working pressure on a machine used by most service stations. Those plugs which fail the test should be renewed. As a general rule, plugs should be cleaned and tested at about 6000 mile intervals and renewed at about 12,000 mile intervals, or before if badly worn.

The HT leads from the distributor to sparking plugs and coil should be examined for cracks and defective insulation. Renew any lead found to be defective in any way. The leads are of the suppressor type with a non-metallic graphited core having a resistance of 4000 to 8000 ohms per foot of lead. To test for continuity an ohmmeter is necessary.

3:7 Fault diagnosis

(a) Engine will not fire

1 Battery discharged
2 Contact breaker points dirty, pitted or maladjusted
3 Distributor cap dirty, cracked or tracking
4 Rotor contact spring not touching carbon button in cap
5 Faulty cable or loose connection in low tension circuit
6 Distributor rotor arm cracked
7 Faulty coil
8 Broken contact breaker spring
9 Contact points stuck open

(b) Engine misfires

1 Check 2, 3, 5 and 7 in (a)
2 Weak contact breaker spring
3 HT plug or coil lead cracked or perished
4 Loose sparking plug
5 Sparking plug insulation cracked
6 Sparking plug gap incorrect
7 Ignition timing too far advanced

(c) Poor acceleration

1 Ignition retarded
2 Centrifugal advance weights seized
3 Centrifugal advance springs weak, broken or disconnected
4 Distributor clamp or mounting screw loose
5 Excessive contact points gap
6 Worn plugs
7 Faulty vacuum unit or leaking line

CHAPTER 4

THE COOLING SYSTEM

4:1 Description

The cooling system is pressurised and thermostatically controlled. Water circulation is assisted by a centrifugal pump which is mounted at the front of the cylinder block and the cooling fan, which draws air through the radiator, is fitted to the same shaft as the pump impeller. The pump and fan and the alternator are driven from a pulley on the crankshaft by an endless belt. The tension of this belt is adjustable at the alternator mountings. The fan is driven through a viscous coupling which allows direct drive through the coupling to the fan up to engine speeds of approximately 1000 rev/min. As engine speed increases further, drive through the coupling to the fan is progressively decreased to reduce fan noise and power absorption without impairing cooling efficiency.

The pump takes coolant from the bottom of the radiator and delivers it to the cylinder block from which it rises to the cylinder head. At normal operating temperatures the thermostat is open and the coolant returns from the head to the top of the radiator. At lower temperatures, the thermostat valve is closed and the coolant bypasses the radiator and returns to the pump inlet to provide a rapid warm up.

4:2 Maintenance

The water pump bearing is packed with lubricant on assembly and periodic lubrication is not needed. The cooling fan and viscous coupling are a balanced and sealed unit. In case of oil leakage the unit must be renewed as it is not repairable. The centre bolt has a lefthand thread and should be tightened to a torque of 14lb ft.

The cooling system should be checked regularly for correct coolant level when the engine is cool. When removing the radiator filler cap on a hot engine, hold the cap with a large piece of rag. Turn the cap anticlockwise and wait a few moments for the pressure to release before lifting off the cap. It is recommended that an antifreeze solution is maintained in the system all year round. Topping up should therefore be carried out with the correct mixture of antifreeze and water to avoid weakening the solution in use.

Every two years the cooling system should be drained, flushed to remove sediment and refilled with fresh antifreeze mixture. Check that the clips are tight on all hoses and that the radiator pressure cap is in good condition and sealing effectively. Loss of system

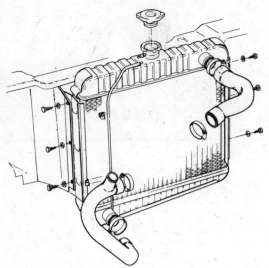

FIG 4:1   Installation of the radiator and hoses

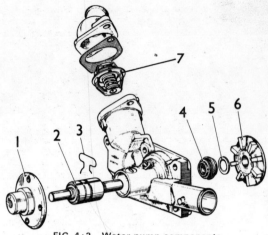

FIG 4:3   Water pump components

Key to Fig 4:3   1 Pulley flange   2 Bearing assembly
3 Spring locking ring   4 Self-adjusting seal   5 Ceramic
counterface   6 Pump rotor   7 Thermostat

pressure due to a leaking filler cap can be a cause of
overheating.

Regular checks should be made on the condition and
tension of the drive belt, as described in **Section 4:4**.

Draining the system:

Place the heater temperature control in the car to the
maximum heat position. Make sure that the system is cool,
then remove the radiator cap. Slacken the clip and remove
the bottom hose from the radiator and allow the coolant
to drain out. Remove the drain plug which is located on
the righthand side of the engine cylinder block. Note
that when this drain plug is finally refitted, the threads
must be coated with a non-setting sealant.

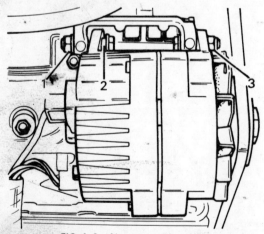

FIG 4:2   Alternator mountings

Key to Fig 4:2   1 Slip ring end bracket bolt   2 Split sliding
bush   3 Drive end bracket bolt

Flushing:

When all old coolant has drained, reconnect the
bottom hose and refit the drain plug temporarily. Fill the
system with clean water and run the engine until the top
radiator hose feels warm, which indicates that the thermostat has opened for complete circulation. Now completely drain the system again before the sediment has
time to settle.

Filling:

Check that the drain plug is properly fitted and that all
hose clips are tight. Leave the heater control in the
maximum heat position. Prepare the new antifreeze
mixture according to the manufacturer's instructions. If
the system is still warm, allow it to cool down as adding
the cold liquid when the system is warm may crack the
engine cylinder block. Fill the system to a level about
1in from the bottom of the filler neck. Check the coolant
level after running the engine for some time and top up if
necessary.

4:3 Removing the radiator

Removal:

Drain the radiator as described in **Section 4:2**. Refer
to **FIG 4:1** and remove the top and bottom hoses from
the radiator. Remove the three screws and washers from
each side of the radiator and carefully lift the radiator out
of the car.

Refitting:

Refitting is a reversal of the removal procedure, after
which the system should be refilled with coolant as
described in **Section 4:2**.

4:4 Adjusting drive belt

A tight drive belt will cause rapid wear of the alternator
and water pump bearings, a loose belt will slip and wear
excessively with the consequent possibility of engine

overheating, reduced alternator output and, possibly, a squealing noise. The tension is correct when the belt can be deflected 6mm ($\frac{1}{4}$in) by firm thumb pressure applied midway between alternator and water pump pulleys. Adjustment is carried out by slackening the mounting bolts and pivoting the alternator away from the engine. If a lever is used to move the alternator, it must be applied to the drive end bracket only (see FIG 4:2). The alternator is fitted with a split sliding bush 2 in the slip ring end shield lug to allow it to be mounted without imposing side loading on the lugs. It is essential to tighten the drive end bracket bolt 3 before the slip ring end bracket bolt 1. Tighten the bolts in the correct order and recheck belt tension.

If the drive belt is worn or damaged, it must be renewed. To do this, loosen the alternator mounting bolts as just described and push the alternator towards the engine until the belt can be removed from the crankshaft and alternator pulleys then withdrawn over the fan. Fit the new belt, then set to the correct tension as described previously. The tension of a new belt should be checked after approximately 1600km (1000 miles) of service, to take up the initial stretch.

4:5 The water pump

Removal:

The water pump and fan can be removed as an assembly, with the radiator in position, but if the fan and coupling are to be removed separately the radiator must be removed first for access to the fan securing screw.

Drain the cooling system and remove the drive belt as described previously. Disconnect the radiator hoses from the pump. Remove the six bolts securing the pump and lift the pump and fan assembly away from the engine.

Dismantling:

FIG 4:3 shows the water pump components. Remove the fan and pulley, water outlet and thermostat. To remove the rotor, use a two-legged puller as shown in FIG 4:4. The puller should preferably have split claws or claws specially machined to straddle the rotor, as shown in the inset. Withdraw the seal and counterface.

To remove the shaft and bearing assembly, release the locking ring by squeezing the sides together as shown in FIG 4:5. Press out the shaft and bearing complete with pulley flange.

Clean all parts and examine for wear or damage, renewing any part found to be in an unserviceable condition. Renew the self-adjusting seal 4.

Reassembly:

If several parts of the pump need renewal, the fitting of a replacement pump may be more satisfactory. The water pump can be obtained on an exchange basis. If the existing pump is to be reassembled, proceed as follows:

The shaft and bearing assembly must be pressed into the pump body so that the locking ring groove in the bearing coincides with the groove in the pump body. The front of the shaft can be identified by its shorter end. Install the locking ring as shown in FIG 4:5.

Make sure that the new seal is correctly assembled, with grooves 1 in the sleeve engaging pips 2 in the outer casing as shown in FIG 4:6. Smear special rubber grease

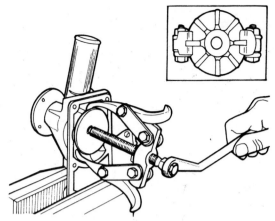

FIG 4:4 Using a split-claw puller to remove the water pump rotor. Inset shows claws straddling rotor vanes

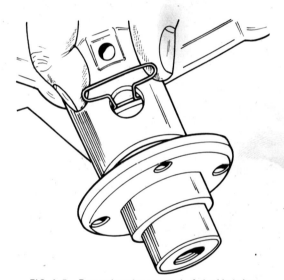

FIG 4:5 Removing the pump shaft locking ring

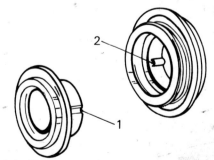

FIG 4:6 The pump seal grooves 1 must engage pips 2 in the outer casing

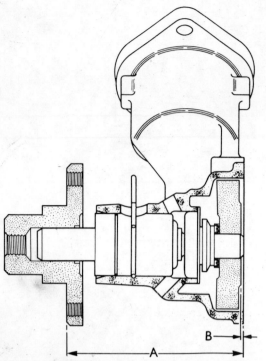

FIG 4:7 The flange and rotor must be pressed onto the shaft until dimensions A and B are correct, as described in the text

on the seal front face and around the body bore and install the seal. Do not put grease on the thrust faces of seal or rotor. Install the ceramic counterface with rubber side towards the rotor. Refer to **FIG 4:7** and press the pulley flange and rotor onto the shaft so that dimension A is 88mm (3.46in) and dimension B is 1.12 to 1.17mm (0.044 to 0.046in).

Install the thermostat and water outlet, using a new gasket. Reassemble the fan and pulley.

Refitting:

Make sure that the pump and engine mating faces are clean and free from burrs. Smear jointing compound on each side of a new gasket, then fit the gasket and pump assembly, evenly tightening the mounting bolts. Fit the drive belt and adjust to the correct tension as described previously. Reconnect the water hoses, refill the cooling system, then run the engine and check for water leaks.

4:6 The thermostat

The thermostat is located in the water pump outlet as shown in **FIG 4:3**.

Removal:

Drain sufficient coolant so that the level is below the thermostat and remove the upper housing from the water pump, leaving the hose attached. Remove the thermostat from the lower part of the housing.

Testing:

Clean the thermostat and immerse it in a container of cold water together with a zero to 100°C thermometer. Heat the water, keeping it stirred, and observe the operation of the valve. The valve should begin to open at 88°C. When the water boils, the valve should be open approximately 13mm ($\frac{1}{2}$in). The valve should close tightly when the thermostat is removed and placed into cold water. If the thermostat does not operate correctly it must be renewed.

Refitting:

Fit the thermostat into the housing, making sure that the jiggle pin is in the highest position in the vertical plane. Make sure that the mounting faces on each part of the housing are clean and free from burrs, then refit the upper part of the housing using a new gasket. Evenly tighten the fixing screws.

4:7 Frost precautions

With the correct coolant solution in use as described in **Section 4:2**, no additional frost precautions should be necessary. However, it is advisable to have the solution tested at intervals during the winter to make certain that it has not weakened. An hydrometer calibrated to read both specific gravity and temperature for the type of coolant in the system must be used, most garages having such equipment. Always ensure that the antifreeze mixture used for filling the system is of sufficient strength to provide protection against freezing, according to the manufacturer's instructions.

4:8 Fault diagnosis

(a) Internal water leakage

1 Cracked cylinder wall
2 Loose cylinder head nuts
3 Cracked cylinder head
4 Faulty head gasket
5 Cracked tappet chest wall

(b) Poor circulation

1 Radiator core blocked
2 Engine water passages restricted
3 Low water level
4 Loose drive belt
5 Defective thermostat
6 Perished or collapsed radiator hoses

(c) Corrosion

1 Impurities in the coolant
2 Infrequent draining and flushing

(d) Overheating

1 Check (b)
2 Sludge in crankcase
3 Faulty ignition timing
4 Low oil level in sump
5 Tight engine
6 Choked exhaust system
7 Binding brakes
8 Slipping clutch
9 Incorrect valve timing
10 Weak fuel mixture

CHAPTER 5

THE CLUTCH

5:1 Description

5:2 Adjusting the clutch

5:3 Removing and dismantling clutch

5:4 Assembling and refitting clutch

5:5 Fault diagnosis

5:1 Description

The clutch is a single dry plate unit of diaphragm spring type. The main components are the driven plate, pressure plate assembly and release bearing, these being shown in **FIG 5:1**.

The driven plate consists of a resilient steel disc attached to a hub which slides on the splined gearbox input shaft. Friction linings are riveted to both sides of the disc.

The pressure plate assembly consists of the pressure plate, diaphragm spring and housing, the assembly being bolted to the engine flywheel. The release bearing is a ballbearing of special construction with an elongated outer ring which presses directly against the diaphragm spring when the clutch pedal is operated. The bearing is mounted on a carrier and operated by a release lever and pivot, journaled in the clutch housing.

Clutch pedal movement is transmitted to the release bearing by a sheathed steel cable attached to the clutch release lever.

When the clutch is fully engaged, the driven plate is nipped between the pressure plate and the engine flywheel and transmits torque to the gearbox through the splined input shaft. When the clutch pedal is depressed, the pressure plate is withdrawn from the driven plate by force transmitted through the cable and the driven plate ceases to transmit torque to the gearbox.

5:2 Adjusting the clutch

Clutch adjustment should be checked regularly as normal wear of the driven plate linings will alter the adjustment in service. If the cable is adjusted with insufficient free play, the cable will be tight and tend to prevent the clutch from engaging properly, causing slip and rapid clutch plate wear. If the cable has too much free play, the clutch will not release properly, causing drag and consequent poor gearchange quality and difficulty in engaging gears from rest.

The clutch adjustment point at the end of the operating cable is shown in **FIG 5:2**. Clutch cable free play should be 6mm (0.24in) at the end of the clutch release lever. Slacken the locknut at the end of the clutch cable. Insert a finger through the unused clutch release lever slot in the housing and spin the release bearing. If the bearing will not spin freely, slacken the adjusting nut a little. Tighten the adjusting nut a little at a time until the bearing is just nipped between the release lever and diaphragm spring. Now unscrew the locknut until it is 6mm (0.24in) away

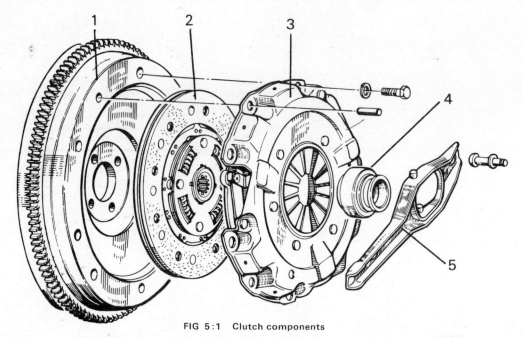

FIG 5:1 Clutch components

Key to Fig 5:1   1 Flywheel   2 Driven plate   3 Pressure plate assembly   4 Release bearing   5 Release lever

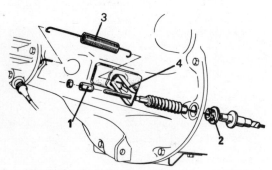

FIG 5:2 Clutch release mechanism and cable

Key to Fig 5:2   1 Adjusting nut   2 Rubber insulator
3 Return spring   4 Release lever

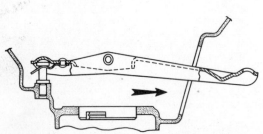

FIG 5:3 Removing the release lever and bearing

from the adjusting nut. Hold the locknut in this position with a spanner, then tighten the adjusting nut against it with a second spanner. Clutch free play will now be accurately set.

If a new clutch cable is to be fitted, remove the locknut and adjusting nut from the old cable and detach the lower end of the cable from the clutch housing. Unhook the other end of the cable from the clutch pedal inside the car, then pull the cable assembly from the bulkhead. Fit the new cable in the reverse order and set to the correct free play as described previously. The clutch inner cable is enclosed in a nylon outer casing which is graphited on initial assembly and should not be lubricated, but a little grease should be applied to the ball end of the adjusting nut.

5:3 Removing and dismantling clutch

Remove the gearbox as described in **Chapter 6**. Punch or scribe mark the clutch cover flange and flywheel rim so that the clutch cover can be refitted to the flywheel in its original position. Loosen the clutch cover screws alternately and evenly until clutch spring pressure has been released, then remove the screws completely. Lift off the clutch pressure plate and friction plate, taking care not to contaminate the friction plate linings with grease or oil. To remove the release lever and bearing from the transmission bellhousing, pull the lever off the ball pivot in the direction shown in **FIG 5:3**. The lever and bearing can then be removed from the input shaft. Remove the pivot ball if it is worn by tapping the ball shank out of the housing. When installing a new pivot ball, use a soft hammer to avoid damaging the ball end.

Servicing:

Thoroughly clean all parts in a suitable solvent, with the exception of the driven plate linings and the release bearing. The release bearing must not be cleaned in solvents as this would wash the internal lubricant from the bearing.

The clutch cover, spring and pressure plate assembly is an integral unit and must not be dismantled. If any part is defective, the assembly must be renewed complete.

Inspect the surface of the flywheel where the driven plate makes contact. Small cracks on the surface are unimportant, but if there are any deep scratches, the flywheel should be machined smooth or renewed. Check the pressure plate for scoring or damage and that the operating surface is flat and true. Check the diaphragm spring for cracks or other damage and the release bearing for any roughness when it is pressed and turned by hand. Any parts which are worn or damaged must be renewed.

Check the driven plate for loose rivets and broken or very loose torsional springs. The friction linings should be well proud of the rivets and have a light colour with a polished glaze through which the grain of the material is clearly visible. A dark, glazed deposit indicates oil on the facings and, as this condition cannot be rectified, a new plate will be required. Any sign of oil in the clutch should be investigated as to the cause and rectified to prevent recurrence of the problem. A slightly twisted driven plate can usually be corrected by mounting it on the splined shaft and using hand pressure to straighten it. Check the driven plate hub for a smooth, sliding fit on the splined input shaft, removing any burrs on the shaft or in the hub.

Check the clutch pilot bush in the crankshaft flange for wear or damage. If a new bush is required, the worn bush must be withdrawn with special tool Z8527, as shown in **FIG 5:4**. Installation of the new bush should be carried out using tool Z8566 as shown in **FIG 5:5**. Make sure that the pilot on the installer tool is free from burrs. The pilot must project slightly through the bush with the nut in contact with the sleeve. Drive the bush 1 squarely into the crankshaft until the installer sleeve contacts the shaft 2. Screw down the nut to withdraw the pilot. The bush is oil impregnated during manufacture and does not require lubrication on assembly.

5:4 Assembling and refitting clutch

Reassembly is a reversal of the dismantling instructions. The hub of the driven plate must be centralised with the hub of the flywheel during assembly, using a spare gearbox input shaft or other suitable alignment tool. Make sure that the clutch driven plate is installed with the marked face towards the flywheel, as shown in **FIG 5:6**.

Place the driven plate correctly on the pressure plate and insert the alignment tool through both. Hold the complete assembly against the flywheel while inserting the end of the tool into the pilot bush in the crankshaft. Index the alignment marks made during the dismantling procedure and install the clutch cover to flywheel attachment screws finger tight. Complete tightening of the screws alternately and evenly to a final torque of 14lb ft, then remove the alignment tool. Lubricate the release lever pivot ball, transmission front cover sleeve

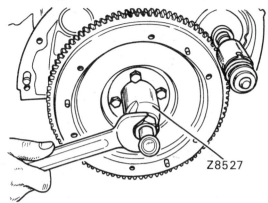

FIG 5:4 Removing the clutch pilot bush with tool Z8527

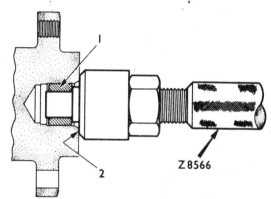

FIG 5:5 Installing the clutch pilot bush using tool Z8566

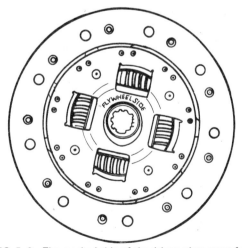

FIG 5:6 The marked side of the driven plate must face the flywheel

and input shaft splines sparingly with grease. Refit the gearbox as described in **Chapter 6** and adjust the clutch cable as described in **Section 5 : 2**.

5 : 5 Fault diagnosis

(a) Drag or spin

1 Oil or grease on driven plate linings
2 Control cable binding
3 Distorted driven plate
4 Warped or damaged pressure plate
5 Broken driven plate linings
6 Excessive clutch free play

(b) Fierceness or snatch

1 Check 1, 2, 3 and 4 in (a)
2 Worn driven plate linings

(c) Slip

1 Check 1 in (a) and 2 in (b)
2 Weak diaphragm spring
3 Seized control cable
4 Insufficient clutch cable free play

(d) Judder

1 Check 1, 3 and 4 in (a)
2 Contact area of friction linings unevenly worn
3 Bent or worn splined shaft
4 Badly worn splines in driven plate hub
5 Faulty engine or transmission mountings

(e) Tick or knock

1 Badly worn driven plate hub splines
2 Worn release bearing
3 Bent or worn splined shaft
4 Loose flywheel

CHAPTER 6

THE TRANSMISSION

6:1 Description

The four-speed gearbox has synchromesh on all forward speeds and is operated by centrally mounted remote control gearlever. The gearbox is shown in section in **FIG 6:1** while its components are shown in exploded form in **FIG 6:2**. The gearbox casing is integral with the clutch housing and is provided with a top cover. All gears are of helical tooth formation except those in the reverse train which are straight-toothed spur gears.

The rear end of the main drive pinion runs in a ball-bearing in the front cover, while its front end engages in the pilot bearing in the rear of the engine crankshaft.

The mainshaft is supported at the front end by needle rollers in the main drive pinion, and by a ballbearing in the rear cover. The mainshaft gears run directly on the shaft journals which are copper-plated.

The synchromesh mechanism incorporates two clutch and clutch hub assemblies, one at the front end of the mainshaft between the main drive pinion and the third-speed gear, the other at the rear between the first- and second-speed gears. The clutch hubs are a press fit on splines on the mainshaft. The clutches have internal splines sliding on external splines on the hubs.

Three equally spaced slots in the hub periphery house sliding keys which are pressed outwards by two circular springs in the clutch hub bore. A pip formed on the outer face of the key engages a detent groove in the clutch bore. Two synchronising rings with taper bores threaded to form a friction surface are located one at each end of the clutch and hub assembly, and engage the synchronising cone on the adjacent mainshaft gear. Both rings are slotted to engage the sliding keys and have external teeth to engage the clutch splines. The first and second-speed clutch has external teeth to engage the reverse pinion.

The layshaft gear assembly is supported at each end by needle rollers on a stationary layshaft. Steel spacers are provided at each end of the rollers. A thrust washer is installed at each end of the layshaft gear and has a pip on its thrust face engaging in a slot in the casing to prevent it from turning.

The reverse pinion incorporates two bushes and runs on a fixed shaft. It can also slide on the shaft and has a groove to receive the reverse striking lever.

The speedometer driving gear is a press fit on the mainshaft and is located immediately behind the main

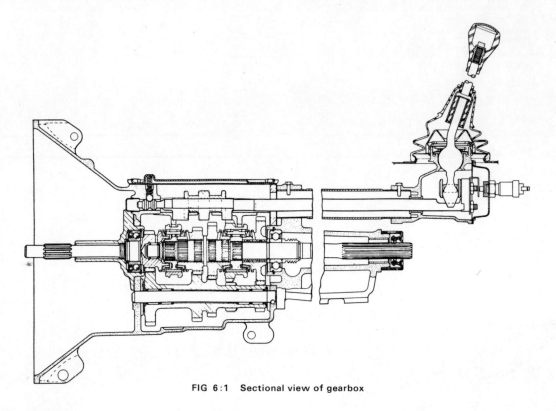

FIG 6:1 Sectional view of gearbox

shaft bearing by a circlip. The driven gearshaft runs directly in the rear cover and has an oil seal to prevent oil leaking into the speedometer cable.

The gearlever is carried in a housing on a tubular extension secured to the gearbox rear cover. Movement of the gearlever is transmitted to a selector shaft, the front end of which is slotted to engage the selector forks and reverse striking lever. A spring-loaded detent ball engages in grooves at the front end of the shaft as shown in **FIG 6:1**.

Two selector forks carried on a common rail in the top of the gearbox casing, and a reverse striking lever pivoting on a fulcrum pin in the side of the casing engage with one or the other of the slots in the selector shaft. The forks and striking lever also engage in grooves in an interlock collar assembled to the selector shaft. This collar is slotted through its length and rotates with the shaft, but is prevented from moving endwise by a pin in the gearbox casing.

When the gearlever is moved to the left from neutral to select first or second gear, the selector shaft is rotated in the opposite direction to bring the first and second selector fork into engagement with the rear slot in the selector shaft. At the same time the interlock collar is rotated so that its longitudinal slot coincides with the first and second selector fork and allows longitudinal movement to engage first or second gear. The third and fourth selector fork is prevented from moving by the front groove in the interlock collar. The reverse striking lever is prevented from moving by the rear groove in the interlock collar.

When the gearlever is moved to the right to select third or fourth gear, the front slot in the selector shaft engages with the third and fourth selector fork jaw. The first and second selector fork and the reverse striking lever are prevented from moving by the rear groove in the interlock collar.

When moving the gearlever to the left for first or second gear its travel is limited by the lower end of the lever coming into contact with the selector shaft. To select reverse gear the lever must be lifted so that its lower end rides over the flat on the selector shaft, allowing further rotation of the shaft beyond the first or second gear position. The rear slot in the selector shaft can then engage the reverse striking lever. At the same time both forward gear selector forks are locked by the grooves in the interlock collar.

The synchromesh on the four forward gears operates as follows. Forward or rearward movement of the gearlever is transmitted by the appropriate selector fork to the synchroniser clutch. The clutch together with the three sliding keys is moved along the hub until the keys contact the bottom of the slots in the synchronising ring, which is then moved into contact with the synchronising cone on the appropriate gear. This commences pre-synchronisation and the friction between ring and cone causes the ring to rotate in relation to the hub, but only to the extent that the slots in the ring are wider than the keys.

At this point gear engagement is prevented as long as there is a difference in speed between the mating cones. As the speeds between the appropriate gear and clutch

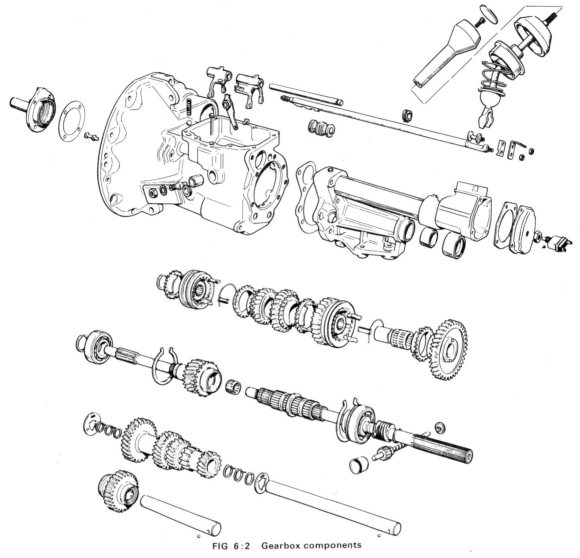

FIG 6:2 Gearbox components

are synchronised, the ring teeth line up with the internal splines of the clutch, allowing the clutch to ride past the ring and silently engage the teeth of the appropriate mainshaft gear.

Forward movement of the gearlever when in the reverse position is transmitted via the selector shaft to the reverse striking lever, thus moving the reverse pinion into mesh with the first- and second-speed clutch gear and the layshaft gear.

6:2 Routine maintenance

The oil level in the gearbox should be maintained at the bottom of the threaded hole for the filler plug, which is located on the lefthand side of the gearbox casing and is accessible from beneath the car. Periodic draining and refilling are not necessary and no drain plug is provided.

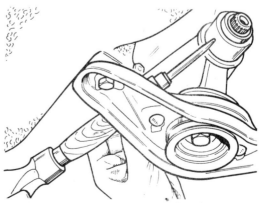

FIG 6:3 Removing rear oil seal

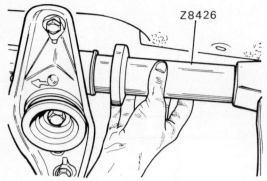

FIG 6:4   Fitting rear oil seal

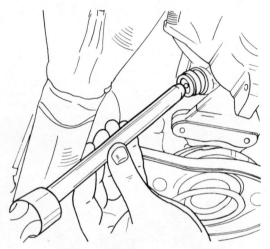

FIG 6:5   Removing speedometer drive gear

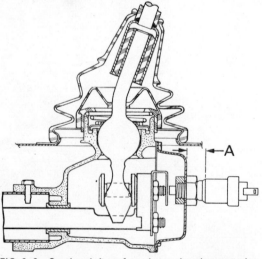

FIG 6:6   Sectional view of gearlever, showing reversing
light switch installation. Dimension A is 7.5mm (0.30in)

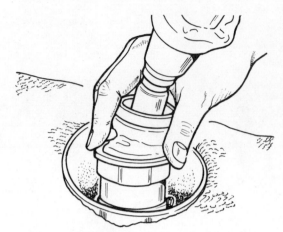

FIG 6:7   Gearlever removal

When checking the oil level clean away all dirt from around the plug before removing it. Allow excess oil to drain away fully before refitting the plug.

Renewing rear cover oil seal:

If oil leakage from the rear gearbox cover oil seal occurs, the seal can be renewed without removing the gearbox, in the following manner:

Remove the propeller shaft as described in **Chapter 7**. Drive off the oil seal using a sharp drift alternately on each side of the seal outer casing as shown in **FIG 6:3**. Soak the new seal in oil and drive it home on the rear end of the cover using the installer Z8426 or similar, as shown in **FIG 6:4**. Refit the propeller shaft.

Run the engine for a few minutes to circulate oil from the gearbox into the rear cover, then stop the engine and top up the gearbox with the correct grade of oil.

6:3 Speedometer drive and reversing light switch

Speedometer driven gear:

The speedometer driven gear can be removed with the gearbox in the car.

Disconnect the speedometer cable from the gearbox and remove the oil seal. Place a tray to catch the oil from the rear cover. Using a brass drift as shown in **FIG 6:5**, drive out the gear and shaft together with the end cap.

Lubricate the gear before installation. Smear a new cap with jointing compound and install by using a suitable lever and distance piece. If the gearbox is out of the car the cap can be driven in using a brass drift. Assemble the oil seal and reconnect the speedometer cable. Run the engine for a few minutes to circulate oil from the gearbox casing into the rear cover, then stop the engine and top up the gearbox to the bottom of the filler plug hole.

Speedometer cable:

To remove the speedometer cable, disconnect the bayonet type cable connector from the rear of the instrument, which is accessible by reaching behind the instrument panel. On righthand drive vehicles, the windscreen demist duct must be removed first.

Disconnect the cable from the gearbox and withdraw the cable and grommets through the dash panel. Examine the outer casing for kinks and fractures and the inner cable for broken strands. Check for wear on the squared end of the cable. When installing the cable, any bends in the outer casing must be not less than 5in radius.

Reversing light switch:

FIG 6 : 6 shows the method of assembling the reversing light switch. Before installation, smear the threads of the switch with jointing compound. Do not allow compound to run onto the switch plunger or it may stick in the ON position. Screw the switch into the gearlever housing until dimension A is 7.5mm (0.30in), then tighten the locknut. Make sure that the wiring connectors are clean and tight.

6 : 4 Gearbox removal

The gearbox is removed as a separate unit from the engine.

1 Remove the gearlever by releasing the rubber boots, pressing down on the cap and twisting clockwise, as shown in **FIG 6 : 7**.
2 Disconnect the clutch cable from the clutch release lever and remove the clutch housing front cover. To facilitate removal of this cover, slacken the transmission brace bolts at the sump bracket. Disconnect the speedometer cable from the gearbox.
3 Have ready a spare sliding sleeve (arrowed in **FIG 6 : 8**), or a suitable plug to cover or prevent oil loss when the propeller shaft is withdrawn from the gearbox rear cover. Support the gearbox on a jack.
4 Remove the propeller shaft as described in **Chapter 7** and fit the spare sleeve, plug or cover.
5 Remove the gearbox support crossmember.
6 Remove the bolts securing the gearbox assembly to the engine and withdraw the gearbox rearwards as shown in **FIG 6 : 8**, taking care not to allow its weight to rest on the main drive pinion and hence on the clutch disc.

6 : 5 Gearbox dismantling

Complete dismantling of the gearbox entails the use of a hydraulic press for the removal of the gears from the mainshaft, so that this part of the work at least must be carried out by a Vauxhall service station. If extensive repairs are needed, it may be better to fit a replacement gearbox, obtainable on an exchange basis. The components, however, can be removed from the gearbox for inspection as follows:

1 Remove the top cover and withdraw the selector shaft detent spring (see **FIG 6 : 2**).
2 Invert the gearbox to drain the oil, and collect the detent ball which will drop out of the casing (see **FIG 6 : 9**). The interlock collar retaining pin (see 2 in **FIG 6 : 10**) may also drop out.
3 Mount the gearbox in a fixture which will hold it firmly but without distortion. The Vauxhall fixture D1157 is available for this purpose.
4 Unhook the return spring and detach the clutch release lever from the ball stud. Remove the fork and the release bearing (see **Chapter 5**).

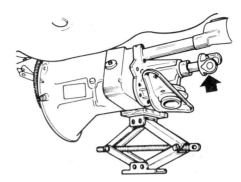

FIG 6 : 8   Gearbox removal

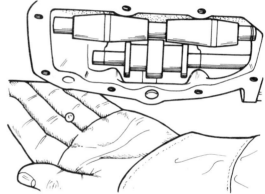

FIG 6 : 9   Collecting the detent ball

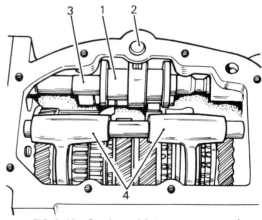

FIG 6 : 10   Gearbox with top cover removed

Key to Fig 6 : 10   1 Interlock collar   2 Retaining pin
3 Selector shaft   4 Selector forks

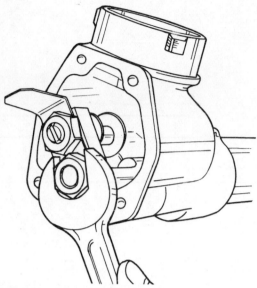

FIG 6:11   Removing eccentric pin and bracket assembly from selector shaft

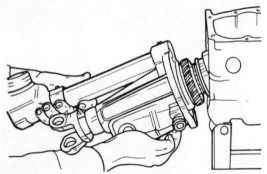

FIG 6:12   Removing the mainshaft and rear cover assembly

FIG 6:13   Removing main drive gear and front cover

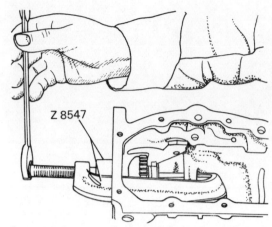

Z 8547

FIG 6:14   Removing reverse pinion shaft

5 Remove the gearlever housing cover (see **FIG 6:2**). Remove the eccentric pin and bracket assembly from the selector shaft, as shown in **FIG 6:11**.

6 Refer to **FIG 6:10** and lift out the retaining pin 2 and rotate the selector shaft 3 so that the key is clear of the selector forks 4 and reverse striking lever, then withdraw the shaft. Remove the interlock collar 1.

7 Remove the rear cover bolts and rotate the cover to expose the rear end of the selector fork rail. Drive out the rail from the front of the cover and lift out the forks.

8 Remove the front cover bolts and move the main drive pinion forward as far as possible so that the mainshaft can be lifted clear of the pinion. Engage fourth gear and withdraw the mainshaft while lifting the shaft over the countershaft gear, as shown in **FIG 6:12**.

9 Drive out the layshaft from the front end and retain the locking ball at the rear of the shaft. Allow the layshaft gear to rest at the bottom of the casing.

10 Remove the main drive pinion and cover assembly as shown in **FIG 6:13**.

11 Withdraw the reverse pinion shaft, using the remover Z8547 or a similar tool as shown in **FIG 6:14**.

12 Lift out the reverse pinion and remove the striking lever from the fulcrum pin.

13 Remove the nut and washer and withdraw the fulcrum pin.

Any further dismantling of the gearbox components involves the use of a hydraulic press. Reassembly of the mainshaft gears involves the use of the press and also the selective fitting of circlips. These operations should be carried out by a Vauxhall service station.

6:6 Gearbox reassembly

Before reassembly, ensure that all parts are clean and that oil drillings are free from obstruction. Checks of wear on splines and similar mating parts are best carried out by comparison with new parts. The main drive pinion should be checked for backlash by inserting it in the splined clutch hub disc.

If the reverse pinion bushes are worn, a new pinion assembly must be fitted. If the gear select shaft pin is removed or renewed, install it so that the punch mark indicating the high side of the eccentric is uppermost.

The rear cover oil seal can be renewed as described in **Section 6:2**. Renewal of the bush however, involves the use of a press and a special tool Z8551. The bush is pressed in so that its outer end is flush with the bottom of the chamfer on the cover.

Gearbox reassembly is carried out in the following manner.

1 Install the reverse striking lever fulcrum pin with the centre punch mark indicating the high side of the eccentric uppermost as shown in **FIG 6:15**.

2 Install the striking lever on the fulcrum pin with the long boss towards the gearbox casing and assemble the pad to the lower end of the lever.

3 Assemble the locking ball with a spot of grease in the drilling in the reverse pinion shaft. Engage the groove in the reverse pinion with the striking lever pad. Insert the shaft, lining up the ball with the recess in the casing and drive the shaft home with a brass drift.

4 To ensure that the reverse pinion is correctly positioned, temporarily install the rear cover to the casing and locate in position with one of the cover bolts.

5 Install the selector shaft and interlock collar with the retaining pin (see **FIG 6:10**).

6 Rotate the selector shaft so that the reverse striking lever engages the circular groove in the interlock collar.

7 Adjust the reverse striking lever by means of the eccentric fulcrum pin to give a clearance of 0.05 to 0.30mm (0.002 to 0.012in) between the rear face of the reverse pinion and the casing. Tighten the nut on the fulcrum pin.

8 Remove the selector shaft and rear cover.

9 If the main drive pinion and bearing have been removed, press them into the front cover.

10 Insert the mainshaft roller bearing in the counterbore of the main drive pinion.

11 A double row of rollers, 25 in each row, is incorporated in both ends of the layshaft gear (see **FIG 6:16**). Both sets of rollers have spacers (arrowed) situated between the two rows and at each end. Install the rollers and spacers correctly.

12 Smear the layshaft thrust washers with petroleum jelly and place them on the thrust faces of the gear assembly. The larger washer goes on the front face of the gear.

13 Place the layshaft gear in the bottom of the gearbox casing, at the same time locating the pips on the thrust washers in the grooves in the casing.

14 Lightly smear the front cover face with grease, place a new gasket in position and install the cover and the main drive pinion. Do not install the bolts at this stage.

15 Assemble the layshaft locking ball with a spot of grease in the drilling in the shaft. Align the layshaft gear bore with the layshaft bore in the casing. Using a brass drift, drive the shaft home, after lining up the ball with the recess in the casing face.

16 Assemble the fourth-speed synchronising ring to the third- and fourth-speed clutch hub on the mainshaft, ensuring that the slots of the ring engage in the clutch sliding keys. Locate the clutch well forward of the

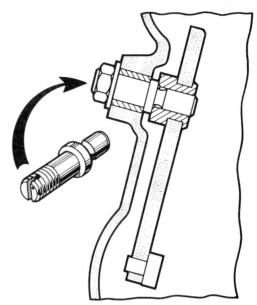

FIG 6:15 Reverse fulcrum pin is fitted with centre punch mark uppermost

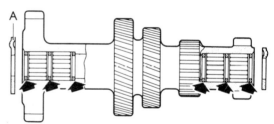

FIG 6:16 Layshaft bearing rollers and spacers, showing the large thrust washer A

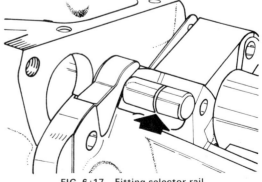

FIG 6:17 Fitting selector rail

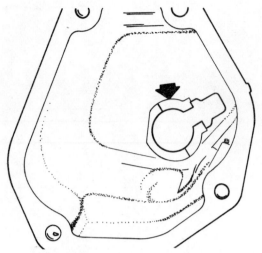

FIG 6:18   Correct installation of the selector shaft bush

clutch hub so that the clutch will clear the third-speed layshaft gear when installing the mainshaft assembly. Withdraw the main drive pinion as far forward as possible.

17 Lightly smear the rear cover face with grease, place a new gasket in position and install the mainshaft and rear cover. Raise the front end of the mainshaft as shown in **FIG 6:12** sufficiently for the third- and fourth-speed clutch to clear the layshaft third-speed gear and rotate the shaft to engage the layshaft gears. Do not install the rear cover bolts at this stage.

18 Assemble the selector forks on the clutches. The third and fourth selector fork can be identified by the smaller boss on the fork. Both selector forks must be located so that the lugs are towards the lefthand side of the casing. Locate the rear cover radially to permit installation of the selector fork rail as shown in **FIG 6:17**. Drive the rail home with a brass drift until it is flush with the casing rear face. Rotate the rear cover to align the bolt holes and install the bolts.

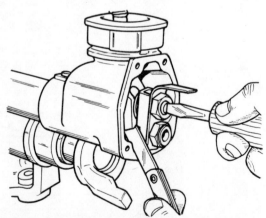

FIG 6:19   Checking clearance between longer leg of gearlever and selector shaft

19 Using new copper washers, install and tighten the front cover bolts. Before installing the clutch release lever and bearing, smear the front cover sleeve and pivot ball with recommended grease. Check that the plastic bush for the selector shaft is serviceable and correctly installed in the selector shaft housing, as shown in **FIG 6:18**.

20 With the two clutches and the reverse pinion in the neutral position, locate the interlock collar over the selector forks and reverse striking lever. Insert the selector shaft through the rear cover and interlock collar, lining up the keys on the shaft with the slot in the collar. Rotate the shaft anticlockwise until the keys are clear of the forks and locate the front end of the shaft in the casing bore.

21 Rotate the shaft clockwise and insert the interlock collar retaining pin (see **FIG 6:10**) and the detent ball and spring. When installing the eccentric pin and bracket assembly to the selector shaft, ensure that the slot in the bracket locates onto the flats on the shaft.

22 Temporarily install the gearlever with the long leg of the lever to the left and engage first gear. Check the clearance between the selector shaft and the reverse stop on the lever (see **FIG 6:19**) and if necessary adjust the eccentric pin on the shaft to give a clearance of 0.05 to 0.30mm (0.002 to 0.012in). Select neutral and remove the gearlever. After adjustment of the eccentric pin, bend the reversing lamp switch contact plate over the nuts.

23 Install the gearlever housing cover, using a new gasket.

24 Install the top cover using a new gasket.

6:7 Gearbox refitting

Refitting the gearbox involves reversal of the sequence of operation for removal given in **Section 6:4**, noting the following points:

1 Prior to installing the gearbox, inject $\frac{1}{8}$ pint gear oil through the end of the rear cover to provide initial lubrication of the speedometer gears and the rear cover bush. In addition the oil seal and felt in the rear cover must be smeared with gear oil. Insert a spare sliding sleeve or suitable plug or cover to the end of the rear cover to prevent oil loss during installation.

2 Check that the starter pinion rubber boot is serviceable and correctly installed in the gearbox casing.

3 Check that the mating faces of the gearbox and crankcase are clean and free from burrs.

4 Lightly smear the main drive pinion splines with grease.

5 When installing the gearbox, take care not to allow the weight of the gearbox to rest on the main drive pinion and clutch disc hub until the spigot is fully home in the crankshaft bearing.

6 Ensure that the gearbox casing locates on the two dowels in the crankcase. Tighten the bolts evenly. Tighten the transmission brace to sump bracket bolts.

7 The rear crossmember rubber mounting is secured to the transmission rear cover by a single bolt 3 (see **FIG 6:20**) which incorporates a retaining clip 1. A large shaped washer is installed above and below the mounting, the lower washer restricting upward movement of the transmission on rebound. As the

mounting platform is inclined 3° downwards at the rear, it is essential that the crossmember is installed the correct way round. On some crossmembers an arrow is used to indicate the front. If no arrow can be found, install the crossmember with hole 2, which is used for manufacturing purposes only, on the right-hand side of the car.

8 After installing the gearbox in the car, pack the recess in the gearlever housing and smear the lever ball and forked end with a recommended grease. Fit the lever so that the longer leg of the fork is towards the left.

9 After installing the propeller shaft, refill the gearbox with a recommended grade of oil. Run the engine for a few minutes and recheck oil level.

6:8 Fault diagnosis

(a) Jumping out of gear

1 Weak or broken detent ball spring
2 Excessive slackness between a synchroniser clutch and hub
3 Slack bearings causing mainshaft float
4 (Forward gears only.) Wear or damage at ends of gear clutch internal splines and mainshaft gear or drive pinion
5 (Top gear only.) Bolts holding gearbox to crankcase loose or foreign matter between mating surfaces
6 (Top gear only.) Slack main drive pinion bearing
7 (Reverse only.) Incorrectly adjusted reverse striking lever

(b) Noisy gearbox

1 Insufficient oil
2 Excessive end play in layshaft gear
3 Worn or damaged bearings
4 Worn or damaged gear teeth

(c) Difficulty in engaging gear

1 Clutch drag or spin (see **Chapter 5**)
2 Worn, damaged or incorrectly adjusted gearchange mechanism
3 (Reverse only.) Incorrectly adjusted striking lever
4 Faulty synchromesh action

(d) Faulty synchromesh action

1 Worn or damaged synchromesh cone or ring
2 Weak, broken or displaced key springs
3 Worn or damaged teeth on synchronising ring

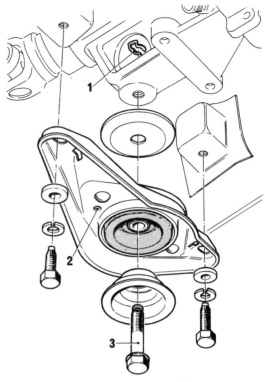

FIG 6:20 Installation of the gearbox rear mounting. The numbers are referred to in the text

(e) Oil leaks

1 Damaged joint washers or gaskets
2 Front, rear or top covers loose or faces damaged
3 Worn or damaged rear cover oil seal

(f) Gearlever rattle

1 Loose cap
2 Weak cap spring
3 Worn rubber bush
4 Worn lever ball

NOTES

CHAPTER 7

THE PROPELLER SHAFT, REAR AXLE
AND REAR SUSPENSION

7:1 Description

Power is transmitted from the transmission output shaft to the differential unit pinion shaft by a one-piece open tubular propeller shaft, this shaft incorporating two universal joints of the trunnion and needle roller type. The yoke of the front universal joint carries an internally splined sleeve which can slide on the splined mainshaft of the gearbox to compensate for movement of the rear axle. The rear universal joint is bolted to a flange attached to the pinion shaft at the rear axle.

The rear axle is of the semi-floating type with a hypoid final drive enclosed in a one-piece axle housing with detachable rear cover. The differential and hypoid gear, and the hypoid pinion, are carried on tapered roller bearings. The pinion extension shaft is splined to the hypoid pinion and is supported at the front end by a ball-bearing in the pinion extension housing.

The rear suspension incorporates coil springs, lower arms, telescopic dampers and a Panhard rod. The axle is located longitudinally by the suspension arms and pinion suspension housing, lateral movement being prevented by the Panhard rod. Rubber bump stops are attached to the vehicle underbody, suspension rebound being controlled by double-acting dampers. An anti-roll bar is

attached at each end by links bolted to the axle tubes and is secured to the underbody by U-shaped clamps.

The items of maintenance and overhaul which can be carried out by a reasonably competent owner/mechanic are given in this chapter, but it is not advised that any further operations be attempted. Special tools and equipment are essential to overhaul the driveshafts and differential components and set the necessary preloads so, for these reasons, the components mentioned should be dismantled and serviced only by a Vauxhall agent having the necessary equipment and trained fitters.

7:2 Routine maintenance

The level of oil in the rear axle unit should be checked according to the recommendations given in the owner's handbook. Note that special hypoid gear oil is required. The combined oil level and filler plug is on the axle housing rear cover. Clean all dirt from around the plug before removing it. The oil level should be at the bottom of the filler plug hole, checked with the car unladen and on level ground. Top up with the correct grade of oil, then allow all excess oil to drain away before refitting the filler plug. Periodic draining and refilling of the rear axle unit is not required.

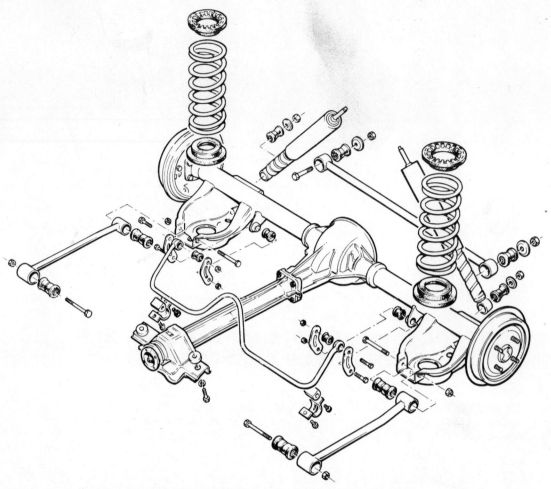

FIG 7:1   Layout of the rear axle and suspension

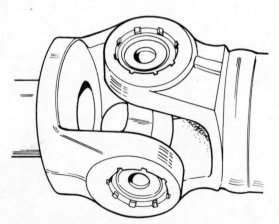

FIG 7:2   Universal joint bearings are staked in position and cannot be renewed separately

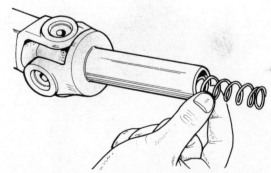

FIG 7:3   Installing the spring in the sliding sleeve bore. On later models the spring is fitted externally

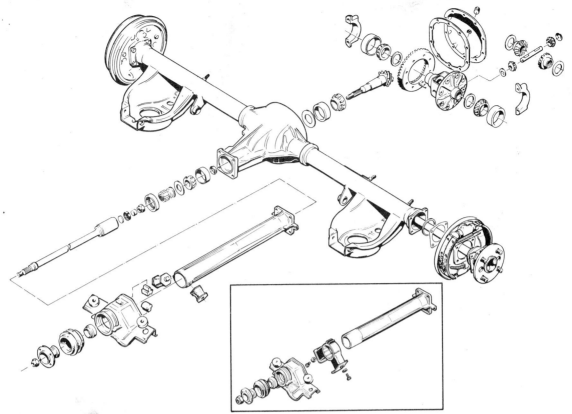

FIG 7:4 Components of rear axle. Inset shows revised mounting on later models

7:3 Propeller shaft

Propeller shaft universal joint bearings are pre-packed with lubricant on assembly, then staked into place as shown in **FIG 7:2**. No servicing of the bearings is possible, so if a bearing unit is worn or damaged, the unit in question must be renewed complete.

Removal:

Have ready a spare sliding sleeve or suitable plug or cover to fit to the gearbox rear cover to prevent oil loss when the propeller shaft is removed.

Mark the relationship between the rear universal joint flange and the rear axle pinion shaft flange with quick drying paint. Remove the locking nuts and bolts securing the flanges.

After withdrawing the sliding sleeve from the gearbox, protect the outer surface of the sleeve by binding with tape to prevent damage. Burrs or scratches on this surface may cause premature wear to the gearbox rear cover bush and oil seal.

Refitting:

Smear the lip of the gearbox rear cover seal with recommended lubricant and ensure the surface of the sliding sleeve is free from burrs or scores. Fit the spring into the bore of the sliding sleeve before inserting it into the gearbox, as shown in **FIG 7:3**.

Align the paint marks on the rear universal joint flange and the rear axle pinion shaft flange and fit the retaining bolts, noting that the heads of the bolts are towards the propeller shaft. Fit new lock tabs and tighten the nuts to a torque of 18lb ft then bend over the tabs to secure. Run the engine for a few minutes to circulate oil from the gearbox casing into the rear cover, then switch off the engine and top up the gearbox.

7:4 Rear axle

Removal of the rear axle is only likely to be called for if a replacement unit is to be fitted. As already stated, dismantling of the axle and differential is best undertaken by a Vauxhall service agent. **FIG 7:4** shows the components of the rear axle.

The spring-loaded seal which prevents oil leaking from around the pinion shaft can be renewed without the need for axle removal, as described later.

Axle removal:

Raise the rear of the car and safely support on chassis stands placed beneath the suspension arm front underbody brackets. Use a suitable jack to take the weight of the axle unit. Remove the road wheels.

Disconnect the handbrake adjuster mechanism to separate the front and rear handbrake cables. Disconnect the hydraulic brake pipes from the wheel cylinders at

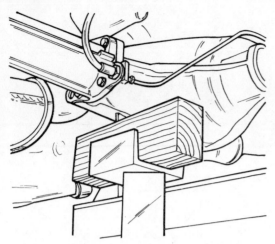

FIG 7:5 Supporting the pinion extension housing

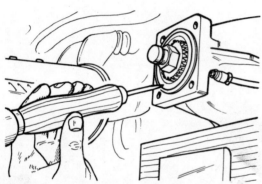

FIG 7:6 Removing pinion extension housing seal

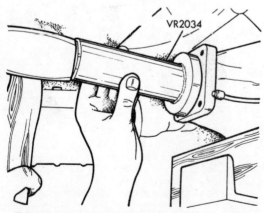

FIG 7:7 Installing pinion extension housing seal

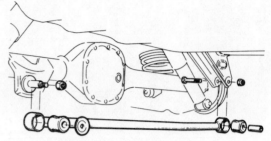

FIG 7:8 Panhard rod removal

each brake backplate and from the rear axle housing. Tie the brake pipes up out of the way of further operations.

Disconnect the rear end of the propeller shaft only (see **Section 7:3**) and tie it up to a suitable component to prevent the front sliding sleeve being disconnected from the gearbox.

Disconnect the suspension arms, dampers, Panhard rod and anti-roll bar at the axle end. Release the exhaust system from its mountings to enable the handbrake cable to pass over the silencer and tailpipe. Remove the pinion housing crossmember bolts, lower the axle assembly and remove it from beneath the car.

Refitting:

Refitting the rear axle is a reversal of the removal procedure, noting the following points:

The car must be correctly loaded as described in **Section 7:5** before tightening the suspension arm bolts and pinion extension housing to crossmember mounting bolts.

On completion, bleed the braking system, reconnect the handbrake cable and check brake adjustment (see **Chapter 10**). Check the level of oil in the rear axle as described in **Section 7:2**.

Pinion shaft seal removal:

Before any work is carried out on the axle which involves removal of the pinion extension housing crossmember bolts, the rear axle must be supported with a jack or stand immediately behind the housing to relieve downward pressure from the coil springs (see **FIG 7:5**).

Disconnect the rear end of the propeller shaft as described previously, then tie the shaft up so that the sliding sleeve is not disconnected from the gearbox. Disconnect the brake fluid pipe from the pinion housing flange. With the housing properly supported, remove the bolts securing the pinion extension housing to the axle, using a special M8 tri-square bit. Disconnect the pinion housing crossmember and remove the housing.

Carefully prise the seal from the housing, using a suitable pointed tool as shown in **FIG 7:6**. Install the new seal, open end first, using installer VR2034 or similar so that the seal case is flush with the end of the axle housing (see **FIG 7:7**).

Refit the components removed for seal renewal and, on completion, bleed the braking system as described in **Chapter 10**. Check the oil level in the axle as described previously.

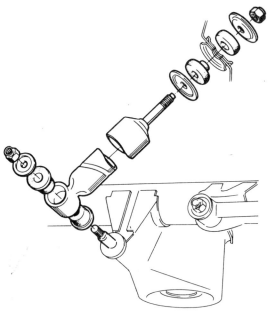

FIG 7:9   Damper mounting details

FIG 7:10   Damper upper mounting nuts

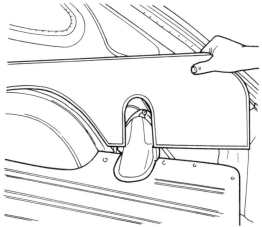

FIG 7:11   Trim panel removal

7:5 Rear suspension

The layout of the rear suspension components is shown in **FIG 7:1**.

Panhard rod:

The Panhard rod is fitted between an anchorage on the righthand side of the underbody and a bracket on the lefthand axle tube. Both ends of the rod are provided with rubber bushes and the end secured to the underbody has an additional internal sleeve.

To remove the Panhard rod, remove the nuts and bolt shown in **FIG 7:8**. Inspect the rubber bushes and renew them if worn or perished. New bushes should be dipped into a soap solution before fitting.

When refitting, tighten the rod to body bolt to 72lb ft and the rod to axle nut to 47lb ft.

Dampers:

The dampers have a rubber-bushed stud fixing to the underbody and a rubber-bushed eye attachment to the rear spring mounting bracket on the axle tubes. Mounting details are shown in **FIG 7:9**.

Before removing a damper, support the car beneath the rear axle to prevent the damper from extending fully. The upper mounting nuts are accessible from inside the luggage compartment after removing the righthand and lefthand floor panels (see **FIG 7:10**). Remove the carpet which is retained by press studs for access to the floor panel retaining screws. As the fuel tank filler tube protector is integral with the righthand floor panel, the trim panel must be removed for access to the protector securing screw as shown in **FIG 7:11**. Carefully insert a screwdriver or similar tool behind the panel to lever out the press-type fasteners.

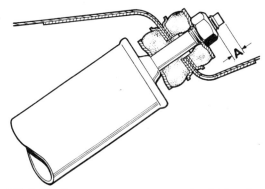

FIG 7:12   Damper upper nuts must be tightened so that dimension A is 8mm (0.31)

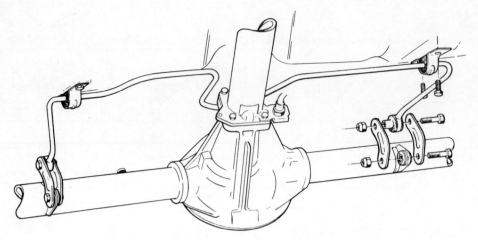

FIG 7:13 Anti-roll bar mounting details

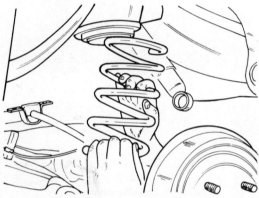

FIG 7:14 Coil spring removal

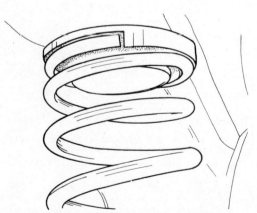

FIG 7:15 Correct location of upper spring seat

When refitting a damper, ensure that the upper mounting bushes and cups are located correctly, as shown in **FIG 7:12**. Tighten the upper mounting nuts until dimension A is 8mm (0.31in). Tighten the damper lower mounting nuts to 32lb ft.

Anti-roll bar:

The anti-roll bar is attached at each end by links bolted to the axle tubes and is secured to the underbody by U-shaped clamps. The clamps incorporate rubber insulators and at each end of the links rubber bushes with internal sleeves are fitted (see **FIG 7:13**). Removal and refitting of the anti-roll bar are straightforward operations. Renew the rubber bushes if they are worn or perished.

Coil springs:

The rear coil springs are supported on rubber seats located in the axle tube brackets and on the underbody. Mounting details are shown in **FIG 7:1**.

To remove a coil spring, support the rear of the body on chassis stands and support the axle with a suitable jack or hoist. Disconnect the anti-roll bar from both underbody mountings (see **FIG 7:13**). Slacken the suspension arm mounting bolt nuts. To avoid stretching the brake hose, springs should be removed one side at a time. Disconnect the damper lower mounting from the side being worked on, then lower that side of the axle. The spring and seats can be removed by pulling down on the spring as shown in **FIG 7:14**.

Before installing a coil spring, make sure that the spring seat is correctly located in the axle tube bracket and fit the spring with the straightened coil end towards the axle. Fit the upper spring seat to the springs so that the step in the seat contacts the end of the spring coil, as shown in **FIG 7:15**. Before tightening the suspension arm attachment, the car must be correctly loaded as described later.

Suspension arms:

The rubber bushed suspension arms are clamped between brackets on the underbody and axle housing (see **FIG 7:16**). The bushes incorporate internal sleeves. Suspension arms can be removed regardless of axle position relative to the car body, after removing the handbrake cable guide from the clip beneath the arm (see **FIG 7:17**).

As special tools and press equipment are required to remove and refit suspension arm bushes, this work should be carried out by a Vauxhall service station.

Refit the suspension arm with the handbrake cable clip towards the rear and facing downwards. Before tightening the suspension arm bolts, the suspension must be set to the correct tightening position. To do this, insert a block of wood, 115mm (4.5in) long, between the axle and underbody adjacent to each bump stop and load the rear of the car until the wooden blocks contact the underbody (see **FIG 7:18**). This operation must be carried out on completion of any work involving slackening of the suspension arm mountings. Tighten the suspension arm mounting bolts to 50lb ft.

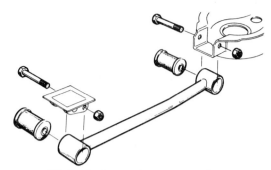

FIG 7:16   Suspension arm mountings

7:6 Fault diagnosis

(a) Noisy axle

1 Incorrect or insufficient lubricant
2 Worn bearings
3 Worn gears
4 Damaged or broken gear teeth
5 Incorrect adjustments in differential
6 General wear

(b) Excessive backlash

1 Worn gears or bearings
2 Worn propeller shaft splines
3 Worn universal joints
4 Loose wheel attachments

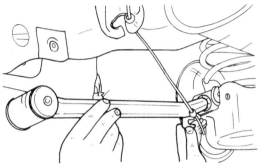

FIG 7:17   Suspension arm removal

(c) Oil leaks

1 Defective oil seals
2 Defective gaskets or distorted casing
3 Overfilled rear axle

(d) Vibration

1 Propeller shaft out of balance
2 Worn universal joints

(e) Rattles

1 Worn universal joints
2 Worn suspension rubber bushes
3 Worn spring seat

(f) Knock

1 Check (a)
2 Badly worn splines on propeller or axle shaft
3 Worn universal joints

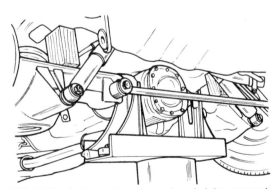

FIG 7:18 Setting the suspension height correctly before tightening suspension arm mountings

NOTES

CHAPTER 8

FRONT SUSPENSION AND HUBS

8:1 Description

The independent front suspension is of the short and long arm type with coil springs and is shown in **FIG 8 : 1**. The wishbone type suspension arms are rubber bushed at their inner ends and pivot on fulcrum bolts attached to the crossmember which is bolted to the underbody. At the outer ends of upper and lower arms ball joints carry the steering knuckles. The coil springs are fitted between the crossmember and the lower arms. The telescopic dampers are fitted between the body and upper arm. Each lower arm incorporates an outrigger which is secured directly to the underbody. The anti-roll bar is mounted on the underbody and linked to the lower arms. Rubber bump stops are mounted on the crossmember to limit suspension movement under compression. Rebound is controlled by the dampers.

The suspension ball joints are packed with lubricant on assembly and sealed for life, so apart from a periodic check on the general condition of all suspension components, no routine maintenance is required.

8:2 Front hubs

The front hubs are mounted on taper roller bearings and the wheel bolts are splined and pressed into the hub flange. A spring-loaded lip-type seal is incorporated in the hub at the inner end and is retained in position by a keyed washer, slotted nut and splitpin. **FIG 8 : 2** shows a section through the front hub assembly.

Jack up the front of the car so that the road wheels are clear of the ground. Spin the wheels and check that they rotate freely without bearing noise, taking care not to confuse noise from the brake with that from a defective bearing. Grasp the tyre at the top and bottom of the wheel and attempt to rock the top of the wheel in and out while noting the play. Repeat the test with the tyre gripped at each side of the wheel. If excessive play is evident, the wheel bearings should be adjusted first and, if roughness is still apparent, the bearings should be dismantled for inspection.

Adjustment:

Jack up the front of the car and remove the road wheel. Remove the grease cap from the centre of the hub. Remove the splitpin and tighten the nut to a torque of 20lb ft while turning the wheel. The nut must then be slackened to give a hub end float of 0.02 to 0.10mm (0.001 to 0.004in). End float is best measured using a dial gauge assembly. When the bearings are correctly

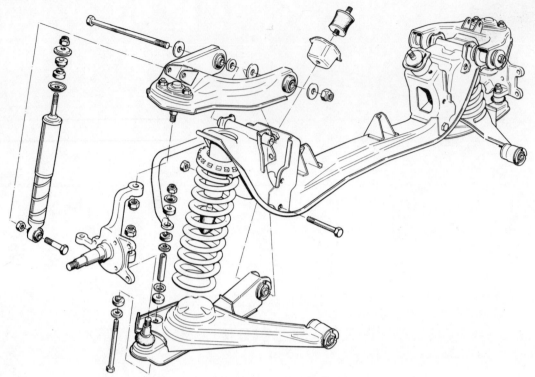

FIG 8:1   Layout of the front suspension components

adjusted slacken the nut a fraction more if necessary to align the splitpin hole, then insert and lock a new splitpin.

Removal:

Slacken the road wheel attachments and raise the front of the car onto stands. Remove the road wheels. Remove the brake caliper as described in **Chapter 10** and wire it to the suspension to avoid straining the hose.

Remove the grease cap from the hub. Remove the splitpin and remove the hub nut. Remove the hub assembly from the steering swivel, using a suitable puller if necessary. Collect the inner race of the outer bearing as it comes free. Remove the oil seal from the hub and remove the inner race of the inner bearing.

Servicing:

Wipe the old grease from the hub and bearings, then thoroughly degrease the parts in petrol, paraffin or a similar solvent. Wash the bearing races separately by rotating them in a bowl of clean solvent. The brake disc must be thoroughly washed with solvent to remove all traces of grease or dirt.

Examine the operating face of the stub axle on which the oil seal operates for scoring or nicks. Light damage can be smoothed with fine grade emery cloth. Check the stub axle for hairline cracks or other damage.

Check the outer races of the bearings for fretting, scoring or wear. If damage is found, both outer races

must be a driven out with a suitable copper drift, working evenly round the races to prevent jamming, then both bearings renewed.

Lubricate the inner races with light oil. Press each inner race firmly back into its outer and rotate the bearing to check for any roughness in operation. Dirt can be a cause of roughness, so wash the bearing again thoroughly before repeating the test. If an airline is used to dry the bearings, do not allow them to spin in the air blast as this chips the faces. If a bearing is defective, both bearings must be completely renewed, including the outer races in the hub.

Reassembly:

If the outer races of the hubs have been removed they should be driven back evenly and fully using a suitable drift.

The wheel bearing must be lubricated with approved grease. Evenly pack the inside of the hub with fresh grease and liberally pack the inner race of the inner bearing with grease, working it well into the rollers. Install the inner race of the inner bearing into the hub and press a new oil seal into the hub to retain the race in position.

Slide the hub assembly back onto the stub axle, taking care not to damage the grease seal. Pack the inner race of the outer bearing with grease and fit it back into place, followed by the washer and nut. Adjust the wheel bearings as described previously and fit a new splitpin. Install the grease cap. Refit the brake caliper,

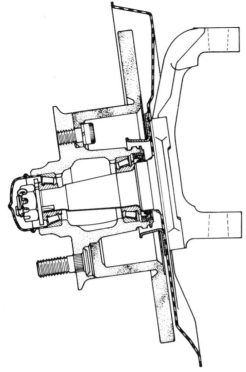

FIG 8:2   Section through the front hub assembly

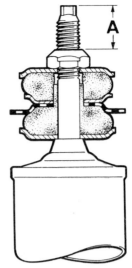

FIG 8:3   Install damper so that dimension A is 20mm (0.8in)

bleeding the brakes if the flexible hose was disconnected, then pump the brake pedal hard several times to take up the adjustment in the brakes. Refit the road wheel and lower the car to the ground.

8:3 Dampers and anti-roll bar

Dampers:

The front dampers have a stud fixing to the wheelhouse panel and an eye mounting to the front suspension upper arm, both fixings being provided with rubber bushes. The upper mounting nuts are accessible from inside the engine compartment. Never attempt to remove the damper from upper or lower mountings when the front wheels are off the ground, unless the car is supported under the suspension lower arm or a spring compressor fitted, as the dampers control suspension rebound and therefore extension of road springs.

When installing a damper, ensure that the upper mounting bushes and washers are located correctly as shown in **FIG 8:3** and tighten the retaining nut until dimension A is 20mm (0.8in).

Anti-roll bar:

The anti-roll bar is connected by means of links to brackets welded to the lower arms. Metal straps and insulator rubbers secure the bar to the front underbody (see **FIG 8:4**).

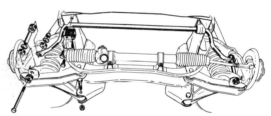

FIG 8:4   Anti-roll bar mounting details

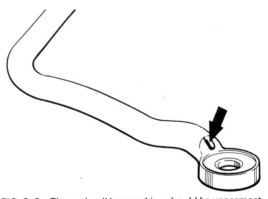

FIG 8:5   The anti-roll bar marking should be uppermost

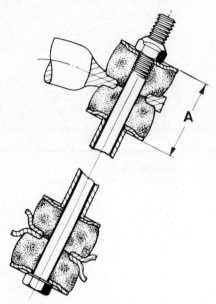

FIG 8:6 Install anti-roll bar so that dimension A is 38mm (1.50in)

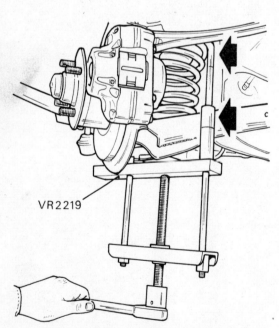

VR2219

FIG 8:7 Spring compressor installation

Anti-roll bar removal is straightforward, but refit with the identification marking (arrowed in **FIG 8:5**) on the upper side and the insulator rubbers with the split towards the front of the vehicle. Insulator rubbers should be smeared with recommended grease before installation.

Install the anti-roll bar ends to the lower suspension arms with the cup washers and bushes as shown in **FIG 8:6**. Tighten the nut until dimension A is 38mm (1.50in).

8:4 Coil springs

The front coil springs are equal in length and may be interchanged side to side.

Removal:

In order to remove a coil spring it is necessary to use a spring compressor such as tool VR2219.

Slacken the suspension lower arm and outrigger fulcrum bolts and remove the anti-roll bar connections from both lower arms.

Fit the spring compressor as shown in **FIG 8:7** ensuring that the hooks are positively located over approximately seven coils. The end of the guide plate and hook painted red should always be to the right as as viewed from the side of the vehicle.

Remove the nut from the lower arm ball joint. Use remover 817 or other similar tool to remove the ball joint from the steering knuckle, as shown in **FIG 8:8**. Wedge or tie the upper arm and steering knuckle away from the lower arm and spring to avoid straining the brake hose.

Remove the fulcrum and outrigger bolts and withdraw the lower arm complete with spring from the vehicle. Slacken the spring compressor to remove the spring.

Refitting:

Refitting is a reversal of the removal procedure. Make sure that the end of the spring with the straight portion seats correctly in the lower arm recess as shown in **FIG 8:9**. Use the compressor tool in the manner previously described when refitting the spring. Fit the insulator to the top end of the spring and install the spring and lower arm to the vehicle. Make sure that the mating tapers are clean and free from grease before attaching the ball joint to the steering knuckle. Tighten the ball joint nut to 30lb ft. Tighten the suspension arm fulcrum and outrigger bolts to 49lb ft when the weight of the vehicle is resting on the road wheels.

8:5 Suspension ball joints

The seatings for the suspension arm ball joints are preloaded to eliminate vertical clearance. The upper ball joints are bolted to the suspension arms. The lower ball joint socket is splined externally and is pressed into the corresponding splines in the suspension arm aperture during manufacture.

Checking ball joints:

Raise the front wheels and support the car beneath the lower suspension arms. Rock the road wheel whilst holding the upper and lower ball joints in turn. If any slackness of the ball in its seatings can be felt, the joint

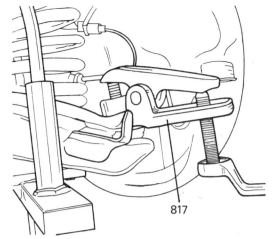

FIG 8:8 Removing lower arm ball joint

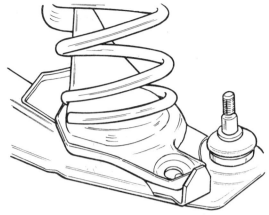

FIG 8:9 Correct position of spring in lower arm recess

should be renewed. The ball joint must also be renewed if the rubber boot is chafed or split, as the boot is not available separately. Rapid wear of the ball joint can occur if the rubber boot is damaged, due to the ingress of dirt and grit.

Ball joint renewal:

In order to remove either of the ball joints, the coil spring must be compressed as described previously. No attempt should be made to renew a ball joint without using a spring compressor.

To remove the upper ball joint, it is not necessary to remove the upper suspension arm from the car. Disconnect the steering knuckle with remover 817 or similar tool as described previously, then release the nuts retaining the joint to the arm. Make a note of the position of the ball joint before removal. When reassembling, make sure that the new joint is installed in the same position as the old joint to prevent alteration of the camber angle. Tighten the retaining nuts, shown in **FIG 8:10**, to 30lb ft.

The lower ball joint can be removed without the need for suspension arm removal but, as special tools and press equipment are needed to remove the ball joint from the arm, the work should be carried out by a Vauxhall service station. If desired, the lower arm and ball joint assembly can be removed as described previously, then the assembly taken to a service station for ball joint renewal. Note that the lower suspension arm fulcrum and outrigger bolt nuts must be tightened to 49lb ft when the weight of the car is on the road wheels.

8:6 Suspension arms

The components of the suspension arms are shown in **FIGS 8:11** and **8:12**. Removal of the lower arm is described in **Section 8:4**, to remove the upper arm, partially compress the road spring, disconnect the ball joint, and withdraw the damper lower mounting bolt. Support the front hub to avoid straining the brake hose, and remove the fulcrum bolt.

Both bushes for the lower suspension arms and outriggers incorporate inner and outer sleeves. On the upper

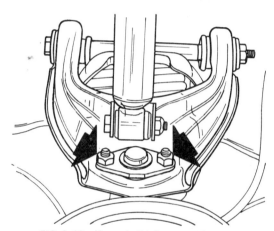

FIG 8:10 Upper ball joint mounting nuts

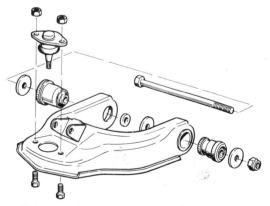

FIG 8:11 Upper suspension arm components

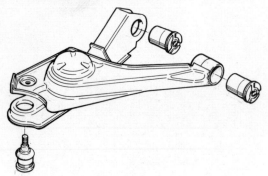

FIG 8:12   Lower suspension arm components

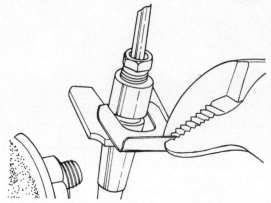

FIG 8:15   Brake hose retaining clip removal

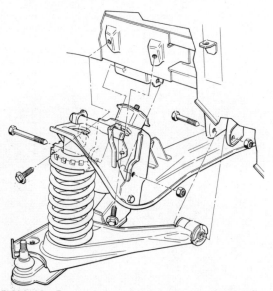

FIG 8:13   Front axle assembly to body mounting details

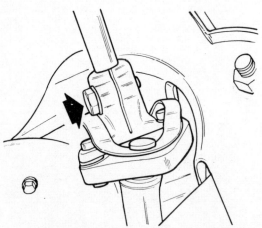

FIG 8:14   Steering coupling pinch bolt

suspension arms, the front bush incorporates an inner and outer sleeve whilst the rear bush has no outer sleeve. As removal and installation of suspension arm bushes requires the use of special tools and press equipment, the work should be carried out by a Vauxhall service station.

8:7 Front axle

The front axle assembly is bolted directly to the underbody, the lower suspension arm outrigger being attached independently to the underbody through rubber bushes (see **FIG 8:13**). The bump stops which limit suspension upward travel are mounted in the centre of the upper spring seats.

Axle removal:

This operation will require the use of lifting gear to take the weight of the engine, and suitable stands to support the body weight when the axle and suspension are removed.

Remove the pinch bolt shown in **FIG 8:14** and release the steering gear attaching bolts. Disconnect the steering coupling from the steering shaft. If the coupling will not slide away from the shaft, turn the steering wheel each

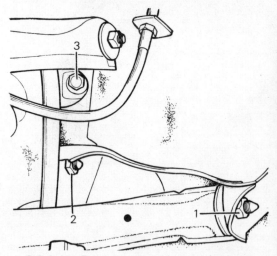

FIG 8:16   Front axle assembly mounting bolts

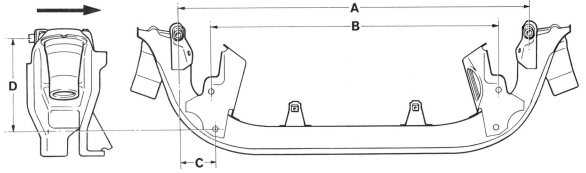

FIG 8:17 Front axle assembly checking data

Key to Fig 8:17   A = 740mm (29.13in)   B = 606mm (23.86in)   C = 73mm (2.87in)   = 195mm (7.68in)   Arrow above side elevation indicates front of vehicle

way to facilitate removal. Do not strike the coupling with a hammer as this may damage the plastic injections in the shaft and make it unfit for further service.

With the weight of the car on the road wheels remove the damper lower mounting bolts as described in **Section 8:4** and disconnect the anti-roll bar to body mountings (see **FIG 8:4**).

Chock the rear wheels, raise the front of the car and support the body at a forward point on each side. Take the weight of the engine on the lifting gear. (Removal of the road wheels at this stage will reduce the weight of the suspension assembly when this is lifted out.)

Disconnect both brake pipes and remove the hose retaining clips as shown in **FIG 8:15**. Remove the nuts from the front engine mounting (see **Chapter 1**). Refer to **FIG 8:16** and remove the lower arm outrigger fulcrum bolts 1 and the axle inner mounting bolts 2. Use a 15mm universal socket wrench to remove the outer axle mounting bolts 3 which can be discarded, as new ones must be used for refitting. Remove the axle assembly from the car.

The front axle crossmember can be checked for distortion or accidental damage by comparing with the dimensions given in **FIG 8:17**.

Refitting:

The axle outer mounting bolts are supplied coated with locking agent and must always be renewed. Bolts that have been in storage for more than approximately two years should not be used, as the locking agent will have deteriorated. Bolts are identified by the last figure of the year of manufacture being marked on the head of the bolt. In the example, shown in **FIG 8:18**, the figure five indicates that the year of manufacture is 1975.

Before axle assembly installation, the axle outer mounting weld nut threads should be cleared of locking agent using a suitable tap, such as tool VR2228.

Refit the axle assembly in the reverse order of removal, tightening the inner mounting bolts to 47lb ft and the outer mounting bolts to 55lb ft. Tighten the lower suspension arm outrigger fulcrum bolt nuts to 49lb ft while the weight of the car is on the road wheels. Tighten the steering coupling pinch bolt to 13lb ft and the steering gear mounting bolt to 15lb ft. On completion, bleed the braking system as described in **Chapter 10**.

8:8 Suspension geometry

Due to the need for special optical measuring equipment for accurate results, the checking and adjusting of front wheel caster and camber angles should be carried out by a Vauxhall service station.

The camber angle is adjusted by rotating the upper ball joint mounting flange through 180°. As the mounting flange is offset from the joint centre, the camber angle will be altered by approximately 0° 50'. Adjustment is carried out by supporting the lower suspension arm, slackening the upper ball joint nut and releasing the taper from the knuckle using remover 817 or similar tool. With the knuckle supported to avoid brake hose strain, the ball joint retaining nuts which are arrowed in **FIG 8:10** must be removed. The ball joint flange is then rotated through 180° and the components reassembled.

FIG 8:18 Outer axle mounting bolt identification

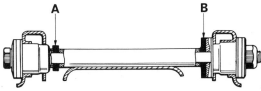

FIG 8:19 Locations of spacers used for caster angle adjustment

The caster angle is adjusted by changing spacers A and B between the upper suspension arm and axle mounting (see **FIG 8:19**). Spacer A has a smaller external diameter and is installed towards the front of the vehicle. Production spacers are 6mm (0.24in) thick. To alter the caster angle, spacers must be replaced by one 3mm (0.12in) spacer and one 9mm (0.35in) spacer in the following manner. To increase the caster angle, spacer A must be replaced with one of 3mm thickness and spacer B with one of 9mm thickness. To decrease the caster angle, spacer A must be replaced with one of 9mm thickness and spacer B with one of 3mm thickness. In either case the total thickness of spacers installed must be 12mm (0.47in).

The method for setting the correct toe-in of the front wheels is described in **Chapter 9**.

8:9 Fault diagnosis

(a) Wheel wobble (see also **Chapter 10**)

1 Worn hub bearings
2 Weak front springs
3 Uneven tyre wear
4 Worn suspension bushes

(b) Car pulls to one šide

1 Unequal tyre pressure
2 Incorrect suspension geometry
3 Defective suspension bushes or damaged parts
4 Weak spring on one side
5 Fault in steering system

(c) Bottoming of suspension

1 Bump rubbers damaged or missing
2 Broken or weak front coil spring
3 Defective damper

(d) Excessive body roll

1 Check 2 and 3 in (c)

(e) Rattles

1 Check 2 and 4 in (a); 2 and 3 in (c)
2 Defective damper mounting bushes
3 Defective suspension arm bushes

(f) Suspension hard

1 Tyre pressures too high
2 Suspension arm ball joints stiff
3 Dampers faulty

CHAPTER 9

THE STEERING GEAR

9:1 Description
9:2 Tie rod ball joints
9:3 Steering wheel removal
9:4 Steering shaft and column

9:5 Steering gear
9:6 Steering column lock
9:7 Front wheel alignment
9:8 Fault diagnosis

9:1 Description

FIG 9:1 shows the layout of the steering gear and steering column. The rack and pinion type steering gear is secured to the front axle crossmember by four bolts. A tie rod is connected to each end of the rack by a ball joint enclosed in a concertina-type rubber boot. The outer end of each tie rod is threaded into a ball joint attached to the steering arms. Steering lock is controlled by the lock stops, which are integral with the steering knuckle, contacting pads on the suspension lower arms. A flexible coupling is connected to the splined ends of the steering gear pinion shaft and steering shaft. The energy absorbing steering column is supported by brackets to the lower and upper dash panels. The column incorporates a combined steering lock and ignition switch.

The steering wheel is a push-fit on the splined steering shaft and secured by a nut.

There are no grease nipples on the steering gear or connections. Maintenance is confined to a renewal of the rubber boots on the rack and pinion gear should these become defective. The tie rod outer ball joints are lubricated and sealed during assembly, the checking and renewal of these components being described in **Section 9:2**.

9:2 Tie rod ball joints

The tie rod outer ball joints are of the spring-loaded type with nylon seatings and it is therefore possible to move the socket in line with the stud against compression of the spring when a load is applied. **FIG 9:2** shows a section through a ball joint assembly. Check the joint by grasping the tie rod adjacent to the joint and attempting to move the joint up and down. If any free movement can be felt in the ball joint without applying pressure, this indicates wear or a broken spring and the joint must be renewed.

Ball joint renewal:

To prevent ball joint housing damage while slackening the locknut, hold the housing by means of a spanner fitted on the flats provided (see **FIG 9:3**).

Use remover 817 or similar tool to detach the ball joint from the steering arm (see **FIG 9:4**). Unscrew the ball joint assembly from the tie rod, carefully counting the number of turns taken to do so.

Screw the new ball joint onto the tie rod by the same number of turns as counted during removal. Ensure that the mating tapers are clean and free from grease, then fit the ball stud to the steering arm and tighten the nut

CHEVETTE

75

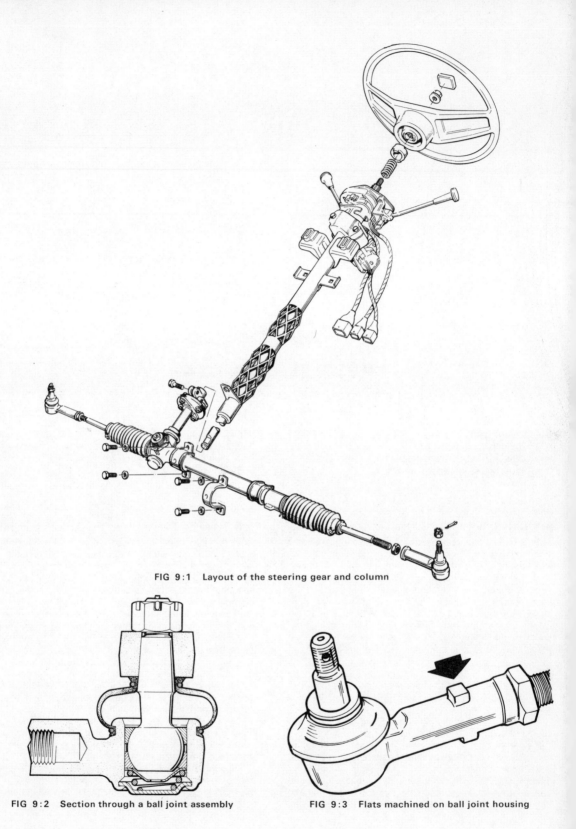

FIG 9:1   Layout of the steering gear and column

FIG 9:2   Section through a ball joint assembly

FIG 9:3   Flats machined on ball joint housing

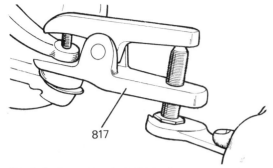

FIG 9:4 Removing the ball joint from the steering arm

securely. Lock the nut with a new split pin. Hold the ball joint by means of a spanner on the flats provided and tighten the locknut. On completion, check and if necessary adjust the front wheel alignment as described in **Section 9:7**.

9:3 Steering wheel removal

Prise out the medallion from the centre of the steering wheel for access to the securing nut. Make sure that the road wheels are pointing straightahead, then remove the securing nut. Pull the steering wheel from the shaft splines. Do not strike the steering wheel or steering shaft during removal or refitting, as this may damage the plastic injections and render the shaft unfit for further service.

To refit the steering wheel, make sure that the road wheels are pointing straightahead and align the wheel with the spokes horizontal and the larger D shape uppermost.

Refer to **FIG 9:5** and rotate the striker bush 1 so that cancelling sleeve 2 and lugs 3 on the steering wheel are aligned. Tighten the steering wheel securing nut to 44lb ft.

9:4 Steering shaft and column

The energy absorbing steering column and steering shaft are designed to collapse in the event of heavy impact on the front of the car or on the steering wheel. The column has a lattice section which compresses when sufficient force is applied to either end. The steering shaft is of telescopic construction, the two sections being held together by plastic injections which will shear under impact. Two pads with plastic injections are incorporated in the column attachment bracket which will shear when a heavy impact is imposed on the steering wheel.

It is essential that great care be taken when working on the steering column assembly to avoid applying any shock loading to the steering shaft column, column outer jacket or mounting brackets as this may cause irreparable damage.

Inspection for damage:

The steering column and mounting bracket can be checked for damage without the need for removal from

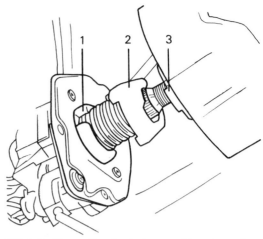

FIG 9:5 The striker bush 1, cancelling sleeve 2 and lugs 3

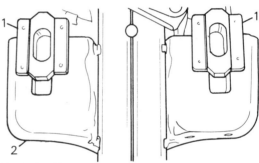

FIG 9:6 Checking the column mounting for gaps between pads 1 and bracket 2

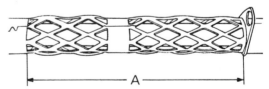

FIG 9:7 Checking length of lattice section of steering column

FIG 9:8 Locations of the steering shaft plastic injections

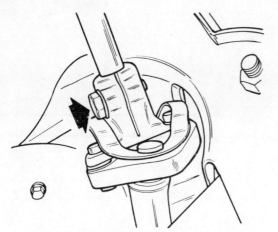

FIG 9:9   The steering coupling pinch bolt

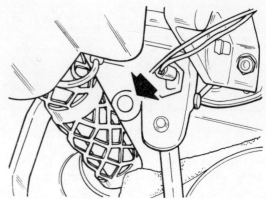

FIG 9:11   Column lower mounting shear-head bolt location

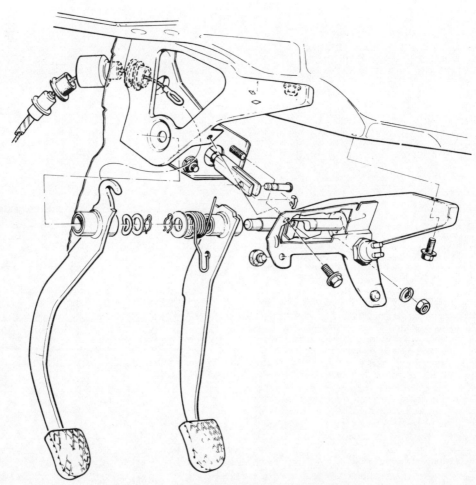

FIG 9:10   Brake and clutch pedal mounting details

the car, but if steering shaft damage is suspected, the column must be removed for withdrawal and inspection of the shaft.

Damage to the column and mounting bracket is indicated if gaps are observed between pads 1 and mounting bracket 2 shown in **FIG 9 : 6**. If gaps are found, the plastic injections which secure the pads to the bracket have sheared allowing the bracket to move forward and the steering column to collapse. Damage to the steering column itself is indicated by bulging or bending of the lattice section (see **FIG 9 : 7**). Note that this section is slightly corrugated during manufacture and collapsing will only have occurred if the overall length of section A is less than 263.5mm (10.37in).

To check the steering shaft for damage its overall length must be measured. If this is more than 982.5mm (38.68in) or less than 981.5mm (38.64in), it indicates that the plastic injections have sheared and the shaft must be renewed (see **FIG 9 : 8**). No attempt must be made to repair the plastic injections.

Column and shaft removal:

Remove the steering wheel as described in **Section 9 : 3**.

Remove the steering column pinch bolt which is arrowed in **FIG 9 : 9**. If the coupling will not slide away from the steering shaft, ease the assembly by turning the steering wheel each way. **Do not strike the coupling with a hammer as this may damage the plastic injections in the steering shaft.**

The brake and clutch pedal assembly, shown in **FIG 9 : 10**, must be withdrawn to enable the shear head bolt to be drilled. Disconnect the clutch cable from the release lever and pedal as described in **Chapter 5**. Remove the circlip and clevis pin securing the brake pedal to the pushrod, then remove the fixing bolts and detach the brake and clutch pedal assembly.

The column lower mounting shear head bolt is arrowed in **FIG 9 : 11**. This can be released from the floor panel weld nut after drilling with a 3mm ($\frac{1}{8}$in) diameter sharp high-speed drill and removing with a suitable screw extractor.

Disconnect the choke cable at the carburetter end and pull it through from the dashboard end to remove it. Unscrew the choke cable locking ring using a suitable tool having two pegs to locate in the holes in the ring. Special tool VR2226 is available for this purpose. Remove the three fixing screws and detach the column lower canopy as shown in **FIG 9 : 12**. Remove the steering column upper bracket bolts.

Partially withdraw the steering shaft by removing the upper bearing inner circlip arrowed in **FIG 9 : 13**, then gently tapping the upper end of the shaft. The steering column lock must be unlocked with the key in positions I, II or III before the shaft can be withdrawn. With the shaft partially withdrawn, release the lower bearing locating clips and remove the lower bearing, as shown in **FIG 9 : 14**. Refer to **FIG 9 : 15** and withdraw the column upper bearing and rubber sleeve 1 after removing circlip 3 and retaining washer 2.

Inspect all components for wear or damage, checking the column and shaft as described previously. Renew any faulty components.

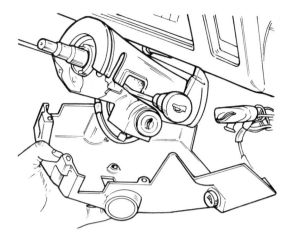

FIG 9 : 12   Removing the column canopy

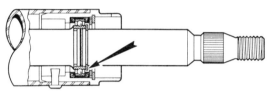

FIG 9 : 13   The upper column bearing inner circlip

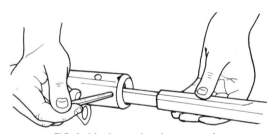

FIG 9 : 14   Lower bearing removal

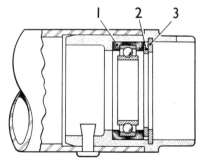

FIG 9 : 15   Upper bearing and sleeve 1, retaining washer 2 and circlip 3

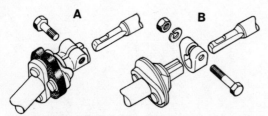

FIG 9:16 Steering coupling clamp details for right-hand drive A and lefthand drive B

Refitting:

Refitting of the steering shaft and column assembly is a reversal of the removal procedure, noting the following points:

When reassembling the column upper bearing, pack the bearing with recommended grease and place the rubber sleeve over the bearing before pressing the bearing and sleeve into the column housing.

Prior to steering shaft installation, make sure that the 'O' ring is installed in the centre of the three grooves at the top end of the shaft, between the upper bearing register and circlip groove.

Lubricate the steering shaft lower bearing felt lining with recommended grease. Work the grease well into the felt and partially install the steering shaft until the waisted section permits installation of the lower bearing into the steering column. Make sure that the pips of the bearing are fully engaged in the locating holes in the column otherwise the felt lining may be damaged.

The steering shaft can be installed into the correct position by means of hand pressure only by pulling the upper end of the shaft. **Do not use a hammer to install the shaft.**

Before fitting the steering column make sure that the rubber gaiter is in good condition and correctly located over the lower dash panel aperture. When lowering the column into position make sure that the cut-out in the shaft is towards the pinch bolt side of the coupling clamp. Coupling clamp details for righthand drive models A and lefthand drive models B are shown in **FIG 9:16**. On lefthand drive models install the clamp so that the pinch bolt is assembled from the lefthand side of the car with the flat on the steering shaft uppermost.

Loosely install the column mounting and steering coupling nuts and bolts, then initially tighten a new column lower mounting shear head bolt to a torque of 15lb ft. Tighten the column upper mounting nut to 10lb ft and the coupling pinch bolt to 13lb ft, then finally tighten the column lower mounting bolt until the head breaks off.

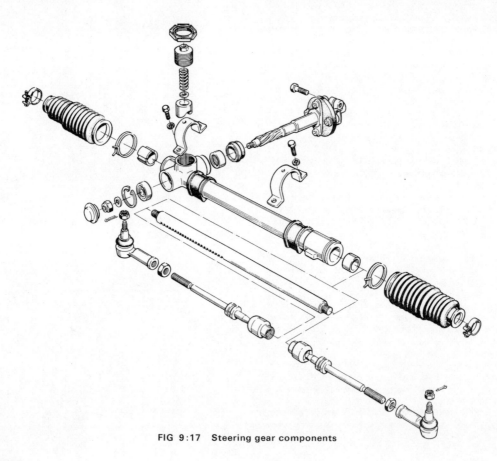

FIG 9:17 Steering gear components

9:5 Steering gear

The steering rack is supported at both ends of the steering gear housing by pre-finished bushes. The pinion is supported in the housing by means of a needle roller bearing at the upper end and a ballbearing on the lower end of the shaft. A spring-loaded adjustable thrust bearing controls the loading of the rack with the pinion. Lock-stops integral with the steering knuckle contact pads on the suspension lower arms to control steering lock. **FIG 9:17** shows the steering gear components.

Removal:

Detach the tie rod ball joints from the steering arms as described in **Section 9:2**, then disconnect the steering coupling as described in **Section 9:4**. Remove the four bolts securing the steering gear clamps to the cross-member, then carefully remove the steering gear assembly from the car.

Dismantling:

Remove the tie rod outer ball joint assembly as described in **Section 9:2**. Release the retaining clips and remove the rubber gaiters from the tie rods. Hold the rack with one spanner and use a second spanner to remove the tie rod and inner ball joint assembly, as shown in **FIG 9:18**.

Slacken the locknut and remove the adjusting screw, spring, washer and thrust bearing from the rack housing, as shown in **FIG 9:19**. Withdraw the dust cover and hold the pinion shaft while removing the pinion retaining nut as shown in **FIG 9:20**. Remove the pinion shaft and rack, withdrawing the rack from the pinion end of the housing to avoid damaging the housing bushes.

Remove the circlip from the housing and drive out the lower pinion shaft bearing. The upper pinion shaft needle bearing may be removed by using a suitable mandrel and spacer as shown in **FIG 9:21**. Place the assembly under a press or between the jaws of a large vice to press the bearing from the housing.

Thoroughly clean all components and inspect for wear or damage. Renew any components found to be in an unserviceable condition.

Reassembly:

Press the pinion shaft upper needle bearing into the housing using a suitable tube. Install the pinion shaft lower bearing and secure with the circlip. Fill the steering gear housing bore between the bushes with approximately 50gm (2oz) of recommended grease.

Install the rack into the housing from the pinion end and position the rack so that it protrudes an equal distance from each end of the housing, as shown at A in **FIG 9:22**.

Lubricate the pinion shaft and housing with recommended grease and fit the shaft so that the slot in the coupling is aligned with the rack thrust bearing adjustment screw. Fit the washer to the pinion shaft, then tighten the retaining nut to 11lb ft and install the dust cover. Install the rack thrust bearing, spring and adjusting screw to the steering gear housing. Make sure that the rack is still in the midway position and tighten the adjuster screw until a resistance is felt, then back off the screw 30° to 60°. Make sure that the steering operates without binding through full movement of the rack, then tighten the locknut to 50lb ft.

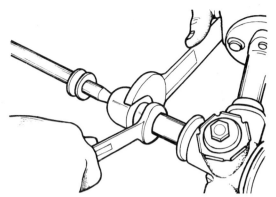

FIG 9:18   Tie rod and inner ball joint removal

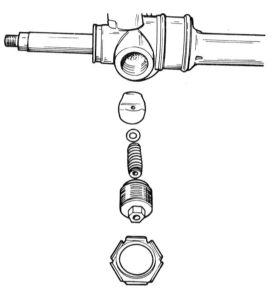

FIG 9:19   Rack and pinion adjustment mechanism

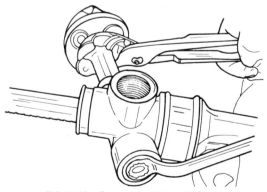

FIG 9:20   Removing pinion shaft nut

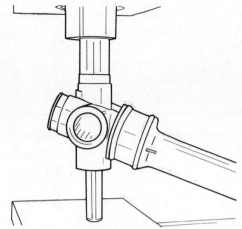

FIG 9:21   Pinion shaft needle bearing removal

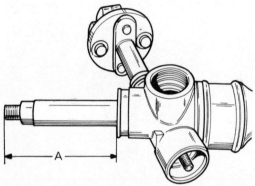

FIG 9:22   Install the rack so that protrusion A is equal on both sides

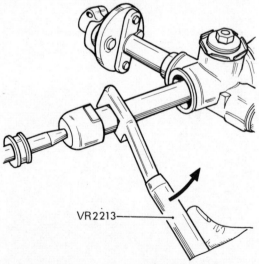

VR2213

FIG 9:23   Staking the tie rod ball joint attachments

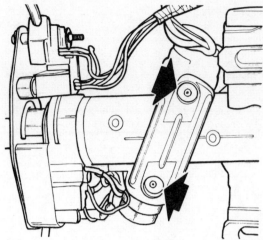

FIG 9:24   Locations of the steering lock shear-head bolts

Install the tie rod and inner ball joint assemblies to the rack ends and tighten to 66lb ft. Use staking lever VR2213 or other suitable means to lock the assemblies in position, as shown in **FIG 9:23**. Fit the rubber gaiters and secure with the clips. Fit the tie rod outer ball joint assemblies to the tie rods, making sure that they are screwed on by equal amounts, as described in **Section 9:2**.

Refitting:

Centralise the steering gear and align the flat on the steering shaft with the pinion coupling flange. Do not tighten the coupling pinch bolt at this stage. Install the steering gear fixing clamps and tighten the securing bolt nuts to 15lb ft. Install the coupling pinch bolt and tighten to 13lb ft. Connect the tie rod ball joints to the steering arms as described in **Section 9:2**. On completion, adjust the tie rods to obtain the correct front wheel alignment as described in **Section 9:7**.

9:6 Steering column lock

Removal:

Remove the steering column assembly as described in **Section 9:4**. Locations of the steering lock securing shear head bolts are shown in **FIG 9:24**. The lock can

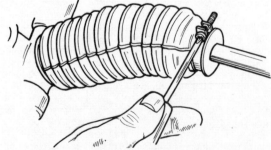

FIG 9:25   Slackening tie rod gaiter circlip

be released from the column after drilling each bolt with a 3mm ($\frac{1}{8}$in) diameter sharp high-speed drill and removing the bolts with a suitable screw extractor.

Refitting:

Fit the lock assembly into position, then tighten the new shear head bolts sufficiently to hold the lock in position. Check the operation of the lock with the key before finally tightening the bolts until the heads break off. Install the steering column assembly as described in **Section 9:4**.

9:7 Front wheel alignment

Front wheel alignment is correct when the wheels toe-in by 12' to 32', which is equivalent to 1 to 3mm (0.04 to 0.12in) at the wheel rims. Although this measurement is best made and the adjustment set by a service station having special optical equipment, an acceptable degree of accuracy can be obtained by using the following method:

Place the car on a level floor with the wheels in the straightahead position. Make sure that the tyres are correctly inflated.

Make a chalk mark on the inside of each wheel rim at the front and at wheel centre height and measure the distance between the two marks. Now roll the car forward by one-half of a revolution of the road wheels so that the chalk marks are now at the back of the wheels and again measure the distance between them. The amount by which the second measurement exceeds the first is the toe-in measurement.

To adjust the front wheel alignment, first slacken the retaining clips securing the rubber gaiters on the steering gear as shown in **FIG 9:25**, to prevent them from being twisted when the tie rods are turned.

Slacken each outer ball joint locknut, holding the ball joint assembly with a spanner on the flats provided to avoid damage (see **FIG 9:3**). Both tie rods have righthand threads. Adjust the toe-in by turning the rods by equal amounts, so that the same amount of thread is visible at each end. Tighten the locknuts and recheck the toe-in. On completion, tighten the circlips securing the rubber gaiters.

Toe-out on turns is a measurement which is not adjustable, this being controlled by the shape of the steering arms. Its purpose is to enable the wheels to be turned so that the inside front wheel on a turn can follow a path with a smaller radius than the outside wheel.

Special equipment is needed to accurately check these settings. If the measurements do not come within the specified limits given in **Technical Data** it indicates that the steering arms are distorted and they must be renewed.

9:8 Fault diagnosis

(a) Wheel wobble

1 Unbalanced wheels and tyres
2 Slack steering connections
3 Incorrect steering geometry
4 Excessive play in steering gear
5 Steering gear loose on crossmember
6 Worn hub bearings

(b) Wander

1 Check 2, 3, 4 and 5 in (a)
2 Front and rear wheels not in line
3 Uneven tyre pressures
4 Uneven tyre wear
5 Defective dampers
6 Weak coil spring

(c) Heavy steering

1 Check 3 in (a)
2 Very low tyre pressures
3 Lack of lubricant in steering gear
4 Tie rod or suspension ball joints tight
5 Wheels out of track
6 Steering column out of line or strained
7 Steering shaft bent
8 Steering shaft bearings tight

(d) Lost motion

1 Play in steering shaft coupling
2 Loose steering wheel
3 Steering gear loose on crossmember
4 Play in steering gear rack and pinion
5 Worn tie rod ball joints
6 Worn suspension ball joints

(e) Irregular front tyre wear

1 Excessive toe-in produces feathered edges on inner side of tread
2 Toe-out produces similar effects on outer side of tread
3 Excessive positive camber causes wear on outer side of tread
4 Negative camber causes wear on inner side of tread

NOTES

CHAPTER 10

THE BRAKING SYSTEM

10:1 Description

The braking system follows conventional practice, with hydraulically operated disc brakes on the front wheels, self-adjusting drum brakes on the rear wheels and a cable-operated handbrake linkage which operates on the rear brakes only. A vacuum servo unit to assist the pressure applied at the brake pedal is a standard fitment. A brake pressure regulating valve fitted in the hydraulic circuit reduces hydraulic pressure supplied to the rear brakes according to the load on the pedal to minimise the possibility of the rear wheels locking under heavy braking.

The master cylinder which draws fluid from twin reservoirs is operated from the brake pedal via the servo unit by a short pushrod and coupling. Fluid pressure from the master cylinder is conveyed to the brake units by means of the brake pipes and hoses.

10:2 Routine maintenance

Regularly check the level of the fluid in the master cylinder reservoirs and replenish if necessary. Wipe dirt from around the cap before removing it and check that the vent holes in the cap are unobstructed. The fluid level should be maintained at a point approximately 12mm ($\frac{1}{2}$in) below the tops of the reservoirs. If frequent topping up is required, the system should be checked for leaks, but it should be noted that with disc brake systems the fluid level will drop gradually over a period of time due to the movement of caliper pistons compensating for friction pad wear. The recommended brake fluid is Castrol Girling Universal Brake and Clutch Fluid. **Never use anything but the recommended fluid.**

Before installing the reservoir top cover, make sure that the diaphragms are returned to their original shape as shown in **FIG 10:1**

Checking brake pads and linings:

Regularly check the thickness of friction lining material on the front brake pads. To check front brake pad thickness, raise the front of the car and remove the road wheels. Look into the front of the caliper recess and examine the friction pads. If any pad has worn to a thickness of 1.5mm (0.06in) or if any pad is cracked or oily, all four friction pads must be renewed. **Do not renew pads singly or on one side of the car only as uneven braking will result.**

To check the lining thickness on rear brakes, the brake drum must be removed as described later. If any lining

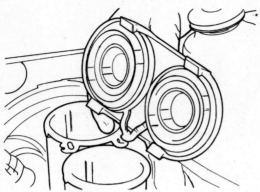

FIG 10:1   Brake master cylinder top cover diaphragms

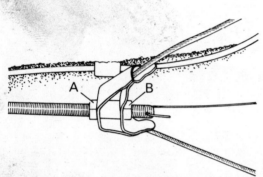

FIG 10:2   Handbrake cable adjustment mechanism

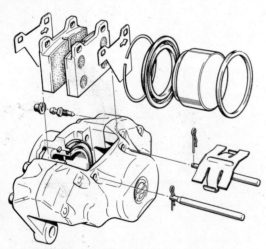

FIG 10:3   Disc brake caliper components

has worn down almost to the rivet heads, or if any lining is damaged or oily, all four rear brake linings should be renewed.

Brake adjustment:

No adjustments are required for the service brake. The front disc brakes are self-adjusting, due to the action of the operating pistons in the calipers. These pistons are returned to the rest position after each brake operation by the piston seals, the seals being slightly stretched during brake application. As the friction pads wear, the piston stroke is increased and the piston will travel further than before and move through the stretched seal a little, the seal returning the piston to a new position nearer the pads when the brakes are released. In this manner, the piston stroke remains constant regardless of the thickness of the friction pads.

Rear drum brakes are provided with self-adjusting mechanisms which move the brake shoes nearer to the brake drums according to the amount of wear on the friction linings. This adjustment will normally maintain the handbrake adjustment correctly, but if the handbrake cable has stretched in service, or if the mechanism has been reassembled after overhaul, the handbrake should be adjusted in the following manner:

A force of 25lb applied midway along the handbrake lever handgrip should raise the lever by four notches on the ratchet. If adjustment proves to be required, refer to **FIG 10:2** and slacken the locknut A. Rotate the nut B to eliminate any slackness in the cable but without causing the rear brakes to bind. After adjustment, check the movement of the handbrake lever as described previously and raise the rear of the car to check that the rear wheels rotate freely when the handbrake lever is released. On completion, tighten the locknut A to secure the adjustment.

10:3 Disc brakes

The brake discs are in unit with the front wheel hubs, the removal and maintenance of the hub assemblies being described in **Chapter 8**, **Section 8:2**. The discs are secured to the hub by four recess-headed bolts and can be detached after front hub removal. The disc brake calipers are of the twin piston type.

Disc brake pad renewal:

Apply the handbrake, raise the front of the car and safely support it on floor stands. Remove the road wheels. Syphon sufficient brake fluid from the reservoir to bring the level down to the halfway mark. If this is not done, fluid will overflow when the new pads are fitted and the pistons pressed back into position.

FIG 10:3 shows disc brake caliper components. Remove the spring clips and drive out the pad retaining pins. Collect the spring retainer. Remove the brake pads and shims, using thin-nosed pliers if necessary. Mark the pads for refitting in their original positions if they are not to be renewed.

Check that the new pads are of the correct type and that they are free from grease, oil and dirt. Clean dirt and rust from the caliper before fitting the pads. To enable the new pads to be fitted, push the caliper pistons down into their bores to allow for the extra thickness of the pads.

Note that this operation will cause the level of brake fluid in the master cylinder reservoir to rise, this being the reason for syphoning off some of the fluid.

Fit the new pads and shims, ensuring that both are correctly fitted. The shims may only be fitted one way up, with the arrow pointing in the direction of forward wheel rotation as shown in **FIG 10:4**. Refit the retaining pins and spring clips ensuring that the spring retainer locates correctly as shown in **FIG 10:5**.

On completion, operate the brake pedal several times to bring the pads close to the disc. If this is not done, the brakes may not function the first time that they are used. Check that the pads are free to move slightly, this indicating that the pad retaining pins are not fouling the pads. Refit the road wheels and lower the car. Top up the fluid reservoir. Road test to check the brakes.

Removing and dismantling a caliper:

Apply the handbrake, raise the front of the car and safely support it on floor stands before removing the road wheel. Remove the brake pads from the caliper as described previously.

Detach the hydraulic pipe from the union on the hose bracket, as shown in **FIG 10:6**, then fit a plug to the end of the open pipe to prevent fluid loss. Do not twist the hose or permanent damage will result. Always unscrew the union nut on the metal pipe first. Hold the hexagon on the flexible hose with a second spanner as a precaution against its turning when removing the hose locknut at a bracket.

Remove the securing bolts to detach the caliper from the steering swivel assembly. Remove dirt and grease from the outside of the caliper before dismantling. If two calipers are to be dismantled at the same time, take care not to mix the parts. **The calipers must not be separated into two halves during servicing.** All work is carried out with the two halves bolted together.

Remove the spring clips and rubber dust covers, then carefully prise the pistons from the bores using two screwdrivers as shown in **FIG 10:7**. Take care not to damage piston or bore surfaces. Carefully remove the rubber piston seal from the groove in each caliper bore.

Discard all rubber parts and wash the remaining parts in commercial alcohol, methylated spirits or clean approved brake fluid. **Use no other cleaner or solvent on brake components.** Inspect all parts for wear or damage and the pistons and cylinder bores for scoring or pitting. Renew any parts found worn, damaged or corroded, making sure that the correct replacement part is obtained and fitted.

Reassembly and refitting:

Use new rubber parts throughout, fitted with the fingers only to avoid damage to the sealing lips. Dip all internal parts in clean brake fluid during assembly. Observe absolute cleanliness to prevent the entry of dirt or any trace of oil or grease. Use the fingers only to fit the new rubber parts to prevent damage.

Fit new seals to the caliper bores, making sure that they are fully seated in the grooves. Fit the pistons, crown first, taking care not to dislodge the seals. Press the pistons down to the bottom of their bores.

Refit the caliper assembly to the steering swivel, tightening the fixing bolt to 72lb ft. Remove the plug and

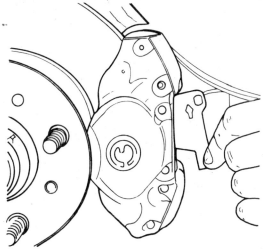

FIG 10:4   Brake pad shim installation

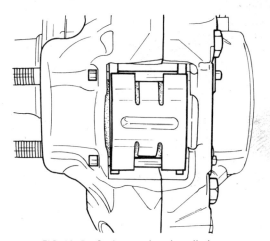

FIG 10:5   Spring retainer installation

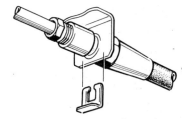

FIG 10:6   Brake hose connection and securing clip

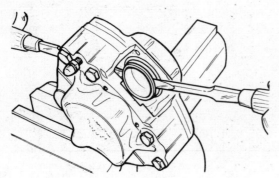

FIG 10:7 Removing a piston from the caliper

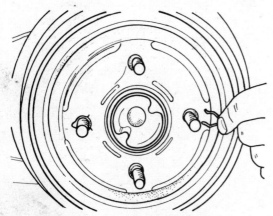

FIG 10:8 Brake drum securing clips

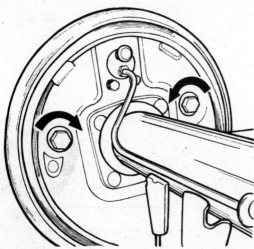

FIG 10:9 Slacken the adjusters before removing the brake drum

secure the brake hose to the body bracket, making sure that the hose has a natural sweep with no induced radial twist. Install the brake hose securing clip so that the bent tag is away from the hose as shown in **FIG 10:6**. Install the friction pads and shims as described previously. On completion, bleed the brakes as described in **Section 10:9**.

10:4 Drum brakes

When working on the rear brakes, chock the front wheels to prevent the car from moving, then fully release the handbrake so that the brake shoes are clear of the drum.

Removing brake shoes:

Remove the hub cap and slacken the wheel nuts. Raise the car and support safely on stands fitted at the rear, then remove the road wheels. Ensure that the handbrake is fully released, then remove the spring clips fitted to two opposite wheel studs, as shown in **FIG 10:8**. As the self-adjusting mechanism ensures that the brake shoes are maintained in a position very close to the drum, the shoes must be backed away from the drum by turning the rear adjusters in the directions shown by the arrows in **FIG 10:9**. The brake drum can then be removed.

Remove the brake shoes, first unhook the handbrake cable then release the front shoe from the lower pedestal. Disconnect the return spring as shown in **FIG 10:10**, then detach the brake shoes. Note that the rear shoe is serviced complete with handbrake operating lever.

Clean all dirt and grease from the inside of the brake assembly. Clean the inside surfaces of the brake drum, using a suitable solvent to remove all traces of grease.

Refitting:

Smear the shoe contact pads on the wheel cylinder, the pedestal and flange plate sparingly with recommended grease and refit in the reverse order of removal. Install the strut and return spring as shown in **FIG 10:10**, fitting the larger hooked end of the spring in the rear brake shoe, which incorporates the operating lever.

Lightly smear the axle shaft spigot with grease and install the brake drum. Push the spring clips onto two opposite wheel bolts hard against the web of the drum, as shown in **FIG 10:8**.

On completion, operate the brake pedal several times to allow the self-adjusting mechanism to move the brake shoes close to the brake drums. Check the operation of the handbrake as described in **Section 10:2**.

Servicing a wheel cylinder:

Raise the rear of the car and remove the road wheel and brake drum as described previously. Rotate the external brake adjuster bolts as shown in **FIG 10:9** until the brake shoes are clear of the wheel cylinder pistons. Disconnect the brake fluid pipe from the cylinder and plug the pipe to prevent fluid loss. Remove the mounting bolts and detach the wheel cylinder.

Remove the rubber dust boots then remove the pistons, seals and spring as shown in **FIG 10:11**. Wash all parts thoroughly in clean brake fluid of the correct type and

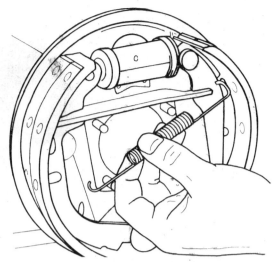

FIG 10:10 Removing brake shoe return spring

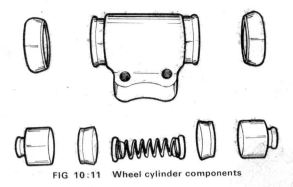

FIG 10:11 Wheel cylinder components

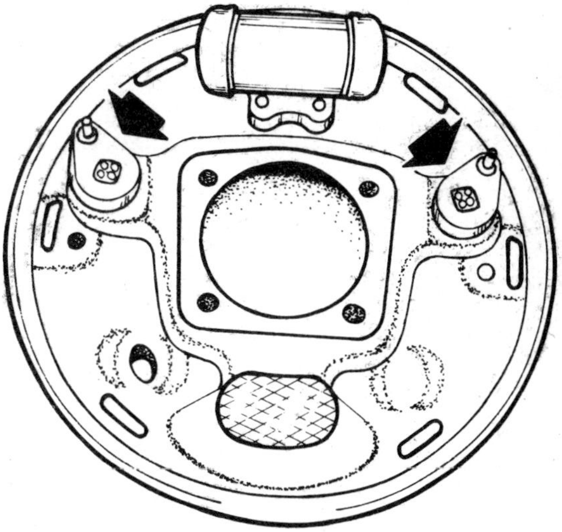

inspect them for wear or damage. Any part which is unserviceable must be renewed. Always fit new rubber seals and dust boots.

Dip the pistons and seals in brake fluid and reassemble them together with the spring, using the fingers only for this operation to avoid damage to the seals. Fill the rubber dust boots with a recommended grade of rubber grease and press them into place. **Do not use ordinary grease for this purpose.** Refit the wheel cylinder and secure with the two bolts. Reconnect the brake fluid pipe.

Smear the brake shoe contact faces sparingly with recommended grease and rotate the adjusters to fully return the shoes into contact with the cylinder pistons. Refit the brake drum and road wheel as described previously.

On completion, bleed the braking system as described in **Section 10:9**, then operate the brake pedal several times so that the self-adjusting mechanism can move the brake shoes close to the brake drum.

Rear brake shoe adjusters:

The rear brake shoe eccentric-type adjusters are mounted on the flange plate, the eccentric pins engaging slots in the brake shoes (see **FIG 10:12**). The adjusters incorporate a wave washer to provide preload.

On brake application, expansion of the brake shoes move the eccentric adjusters and on release correct shoe-to-drum clearance is maintained as the shoe return springs have insufficient tension to overcome the preload within the adjusters. The adjusters must not be dismantled or lubricated.

To check adjuster preload, remove the brake shoes as described previously and use a torque wrench to rotate the adjusters as shown in **FIG 10:9**. The force needed to rotate an adjuster should be between 27 and 35lb in. If adjuster preload is below the specified limit, a new brake flange plate will be required. As this work requires the removal of the axle shaft and requires the selective fitting of shims during reassembly, the work should be carried out by a Vauxhall service station.

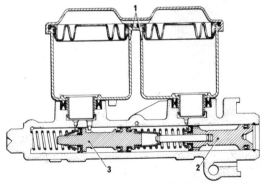

FIG 10:12 Rear brake shoe adjusters are integral with the flange plate

FIG 10:13 Section view of the master cylinder

Key to Fig 10:13   1 Fluid reservoir   2 Primary piston
3 Secondary piston

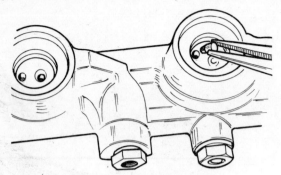

FIG 10:14   Stop pin removal

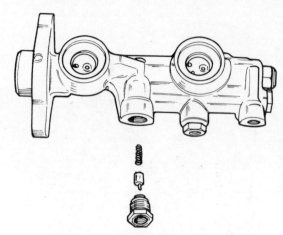

FIG 10:17   Check valve and spring removal

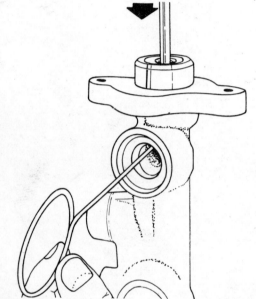

FIG 10:15   Retaining the primary piston against spring pressure

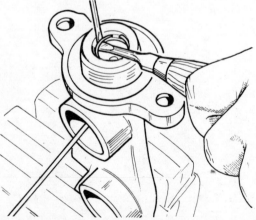

FIG₁ 10:16   Primary piston retainer ring

10:5 The master cylinder

The tandem master cylinder incorporates two pistons operating in a common bore (see **FIG 10:13**). Two separate reservoirs 1 are clipped together and secured to the master cylinder body, fluid being fed to the cylinder by two sets of drillings each comprising a feed port and a bypass port thus providing an independent supply for each piston. The primary piston 2 operates the rear brakes through a check valve in the outlet port. The secondary piston 3 operates the front brakes through two separate pipes, one to the lefthand and one to the right-hand brake unit. Should failure occur in either system, the other system will provide effective braking power although brake pedal travel will be increased. However, the fault is serious and should be given immediate attention.

The reservoir top cover incorporates two diaphragms which prevent the entry of dirt or moisture into the brake fluid. The upper face of each diaphragm is vented through the reservoir cover and as the brake fluid level drops the diaphragm deforms and is drawn into the reservoir. A pressure warning lamp switch contact head is screwed into the side of the master cylinder between the primary and secondary outlets. The switch is actuated by a double-ended piston contained in a separate bore in the cylinder casting. The warning lamp bulb should light when the parking brake is applied with the ignition switched on, this being the normal procedure for checking bulb operation. If the bulb operates when the footbrake is pressed, it indicates a fault in one or other of the brake circuits which should be traced and rectified immediately.

Master cylinder removal:

Detach the two fluid pipes from the master cylinder, plugging or taping the ends of the pipes to prevent the entry of dirt. Disconnect the switch cable. Remove the nuts securing the master cylinder in position then lift the unit from the car. Remove the top cover and empty the contents of the master cylinder reservoirs into a waste container.

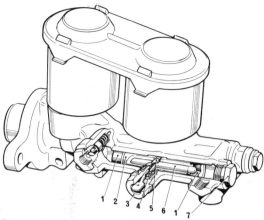

FIG 10:18 Pressure warning lamp actuator components

Key to Fig 10:18   1 Diaphragms   2 Carrier   3 Contact head   4 Pin   5 Carrier retainer   6 Actuator piston   7 Plug

Dismantling:

Remove the retaining clips from the bottom of each reservoir, then remove the reservoirs and seals from the master cylinder body. Withdraw the stop pin from the locating hole as shown in **FIG 10:14**. Depress the primary piston approximately 10mm (0.40in) and insert a length of wire into the primary piston bypass hole to hold the piston away from the retainer ring, as shown in **FIG 10:15**. With the piston held down, remove the retainer ring as shown in **FIG 10:16** then remove the piece of wire and withdraw the primary piston. The secondary piston and spring may now be removed by tapping the cylinder body on a wooden block.

Remove the secondary port connector and withdraw the check valve and spring (see **FIG 10:17**). To remove the pressure warning lamp actuator piston, refer to **FIG 10:18**. Remove the contact head 3, pin 4, carrier retainer 5 and plug 7, then tap the cylinder on a wooden block to remove the piston 6, carrier 2 and diaphragms 1.

To dismantle the primary piston, use special tool VR2225 or other suitable means to compress the spring, as shown in **FIG 10:19**. Screw the two parts of the tool together then remove the locking ring from the rod as shown in **FIG 10:20**. Unscrew the tool and remove the piston and spring.

Servicing:

Wash all parts in commercial alcohol, methylated spirits or approved brake fluid. **Use no other cleaner or solvent on brake hydraulic system components.** Inspect the pistons and cylinder bore for score marks and inspect all parts for wear or damage. Renew any faulty parts. Always use new rubber seals and new locking rings.

Reassembly:

Observe absolute cleanliness to prevent the entry of dirt or any trace of oil or grease. Use fingers only to fit the new rubber piston seals to prevent damage. Wet all internal parts with clean brake fluid during reassembly.

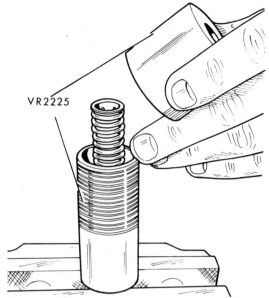

FIG 10:19   A special tool for compressing primary piston spring

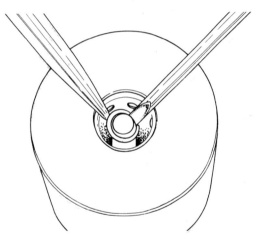

FIG 10:20   Removing primary piston locking ring

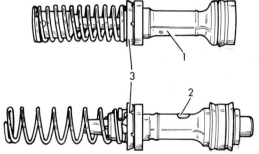

FIG 10:21   Primary piston 1, secondary piston 2 and seals 3

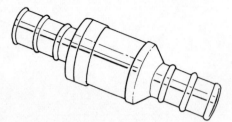

FIG 10:22   Vacuum servo check valve

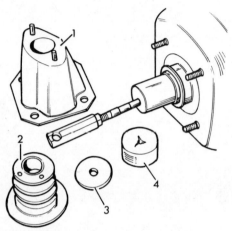

FIG 10:23   Vacuum servo filter assembly

Key to Fig 10:23   1 Mounting bracket   2 Rubber boot
3 Retainer felt   4 Filter

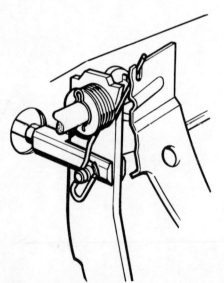

FIG 10:24   Brake pedal return spring and pushrod
installation

Take great care not to turn back the lips of the piston seals when installing them in the cylinder bores.

The seals should be fitted to the primary piston 1 and secondary piston 2 as shown in **FIG 10:21**, making sure that the seal protector shims are fitted behind the front seals 3 of each piston. Use the compressor tool to compress the primary piston return spring and fit a new locking ring to the piston rod. Fit the pistons into the cylinder body then depress the primary piston and retain with a piece of wire as shown in **FIG 10:15**. Fit a new retainer ring into the groove then remove the wire.

When fitting the warning lamp actuator piston, refer to **FIG 10:18**. Install the piston 6 to carrier 2 ensuring that the holes are aligned, then install diaphragms 1. Install the carrier to the master cylinder body, then assemble retainer 5, pin 4 and contact head 3. Place a new sealing washer on the end plug 7.

Install the spring and check valve to the master cylinder body and tighten the secondary port connector to 27lb ft. Install the stop pin. Smear the reservoir sealing rings with brake fluid and fit the reservoirs, making sure that the retaining clips are correctly located. Ensure that the diaphragms are returned to their original shape before refitting the reservoir cover.

Refitting:

This is a reversal of the removal procedure. On completion, fill the fluid reservoirs to the correct level then bleed the brakes as described in **Section 10:9**. Apply heavy pressure to the brake pedal and hold for at least 10 seconds, before examining the master cylinder for any signs of fluid leakage. Road test to check the operation of the brakes.

10:6 Vacuum servo unit

The vacuum servo unit operates to assist the pressure applied at the brake pedal and so reduce braking effort. The vacuum cylinder in the servo is connected to the engine inlet manifold by a hose. The vacuum servo unit is a sealed assembly and, if it is faulty or inoperative, a new unit must be fitted.

Testing:

To test the servo unit, switch off the engine and pump the brake pedal several times to exhaust all vacuum from the unit. Hold a steady light pressure on the brake pedal and start the engine. If the servo is working properly, the brake pedal will move further down without further foot pressure, due to the build-up of vacuum in the system.

With the brakes off, run the engine to medium speed and turn off the ignition, immediately closing the throttle. This builds up a vacuum in the system. Wait one to two minutes, then try the brake action with the engine still switched off. If not vacuum assisted for two or three operations, the servo check valve is faulty. Poor overall performance of the vacuum servo unit can be caused by a clogged air filter.

Check valve renewal:

Remove and discard the old check valve, which is fitted in the hose between the servo unit and the inlet manifold. Make sure that the hose is clear, then fit a new check valve with the arrow on the valve body pointing towards the inlet manifold and the white section of the valve towards the servo (see **FIG 10:22**).

Air filter renewal:

Remove the master cylinder as described in **Section 10:5**. Disconnect the pushrod clevis from the brake pedal (see **FIG 10:24**). Remove the retaining nuts and detach the servo unit from the car.

Refer to **FIG 10:23**. Access to the filter 4 is gained by withdrawing the mounting bracket 1, rubber boot 2 and retainer felt 3. When fitting the new filter, ensure that the rubber boot is located correctly over the end cover.

Refit the servo unit and master cylinder in the reverse order of removal. Adjust the pushrod clevis until pedal free travel is 6 to 9mm (0.24 to 0.35in) measured at the pedal pad. Lubricate the clevis and pin with recommended grease, then push the pin through from the righthand side and install the circlip. Locate the brake pedal return spring in the notch on the pedal support bracket and in the groove in the clevis pin as shown in **FIG 10:24**.

10:7 Pressure regulating valve

The fluid pressure regulating valve is shown in **FIG 10:25**. On lefthand drive models, fluid pressure to the front brake calipers is sensed as it passes through ports A and B. On righthand drive models a bleed screw is installed in port B and front brake fluid pressure is sensed through port A. Fluid pressure to the rear brakes enters the valves through port C and the modified pressure leaves the valve through port D.

As pressure on the footbrake pedal increases, front and rear brake line pressures increase at the same rate until valve cut-in pressure is reached. From this point, front brake line pressure continues to increase at the same rate but the valve modifies the rear brake line pressure so that the rate of increase in pressure is reduced, thereby reducing the possibility of the rear brakes locking. Should a failure occur in the rear brake pressure system, full pressure will still be maintained to the front brakes. However, the valve is constructed in a manner which permits the reducing characteristic of the valve to be bypassed should the failure in front brake pressure occur, thereby delivering full pressure to the rear brakes. No attempt should be made to dismantle the valve if it is faulty, as it is serviced as a complete unit only. Removal and refitting of the valve is a straightforward procedure, bleeding the brakes on completion as described in **Section 10:9**. Note that on righthand drive models, air must be bled from the pressure regulating valve bleed screw after bleeding the remainder of the system.

10:8 The handbrake

The handbrake lever is bolted to a plate welded to the underside of the transmission tunnel (see **FIG 10:26**). The handbrake warning light switch (arrowed) is attached to the mounting bracket and actuated by the lever pawl. Access to the lever mounting bolts and warning light switch cable connector and grommet can be gained after removing the lefthand front seat and raising the carpet.

The handbrake lever is connected to the rear cable equaliser by means of a relay rod. The one-piece rear

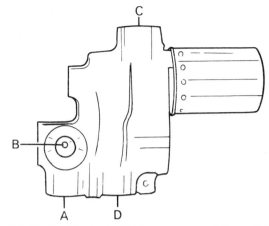

FIG 10:25 The brake fluid pressure regulating valve

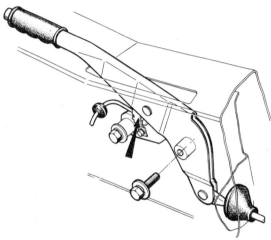

FIG 10:26 Handbrake lever mounting details. The warning light switch is arrowed

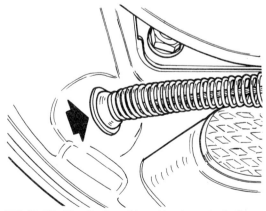

FIG 10:27 Handbrake cable guide at rear brake flange plate

handbrake cable passes through the equaliser, means for cable adjustment being provided as described in **Section 10:2**. Nylon cable guides are located in brackets welded to the underbody and rear suspension lower arms. Eye-type connectors at each end of the cable hook into the brake shoe operating levers. A cable guide, which also acts as a stop for the cable return spring, is secured to each rear brake flange plate by an E-clip (see **FIG 10:27**). To gain access to the E-clip, the forward brake shoe must be removed as described in **Section 10:4**.

10:9 Bleeding the system

This is not routine maintenance and is only necessary if air has entered the hydraulic system due to parts being dismantled, or because the level in the master cylinder supply reservoir has been allowed to drop too low. The need for bleeding is indicated by a spongy feeling at the brake pedal accompanied by poor braking performance. Each brake must be bled in turn, starting with the one furthest from the master cylinder and finishing with the one nearest the master cylinder. **Vacuum must be exhausted from the servo by depressing the brake pedal several times before starting the work and the engine must not be run whilst bleeding is carried out. Do not attempt to bleed the brakes with any drum or caliper removed.**

Remove the reservoir cap and top up both reservoirs to the correct level with approved brake fluid. Clean dirt from around the first bleed screw and remove the rubber dust cap. Fit a length of rubber or plastic tube to the screw and lead the free end of the tube into a clean glass jar containing a small amount of approved brake fluid. The end of the tube must remain immersed in the fluid during the bleeding operation.

Unscrew the bleed screw about half a turn and have an assistant depress the brake pedal fully. With the pedal held down tighten the bleed screw. Allow the pedal to return fully and wait a few seconds for the master cylinder to refill with fluid before repeating the operation. Continue operating the pedal in this manner until no air bubbles can be seen in the fluid flowing into the jar, then hold the pedal against the floor on a downstroke while the bleed valve is tightened. **Do not overtighten.**

At frequent intervals during the operation, check the level of the fluid in the reservoir, topping up as needed. If the level drops too low air will enter the system and the operation will have to be restarted.

Remove the bleed tube, refit the dust cap and repeat the operation on each other brake unit in turn.

When all four brakes have been bled on righthand drive models, carry out a similar bleeding operation at the bleed screw provided on the pressure regulating valve (see **FIG 10:25**).

On completion, top up the fluid to the correct level. Discard all used fluid. Always store brake fluid in clean sealed containers to avoid air or moisture contamination.

10:10 Fault diagnosis

(a) Spongy pedal

1 Leak in the system
2 Worn master cylinder
3 Leaking wheel or caliper cylinders
4 Air in the fluid system
5 Gaps between brake shoes and underside of linings

(b) Excessive pedal movement

1 Check 1 and 4 in (a)
2 Excessive lining or pad wear
3 Very low fluid level in supply reservoir

(c) Brakes grab or pull to one side

1 Distorted discs or drums
2 Wet or oily pads or linings
3 Loose flange plate or caliper
4 Disc or hub loose
5 Worn suspension or steering connections
6 Mixed linings of different grades
7 Uneven tyre pressures
8 Broken shoe return springs
9 Seized handbrake cable
10 Seized wheel cylinder or caliper piston

(d) Brakes partly or fully locked on

1 Swollen pads or linings
2 Damaged brake pipes preventing fluid return
3 Master cylinder compensating hole blocked
4 Master cylinder piston seized
5 Brake or pedal return spring broken
6 Dirt in the hydraulic system
7 Seized wheel cylinder or caliper piston
8 Seized drum brake adjusters
9 Seized handbrake mechanism or cable

(e) Brake failure

1 Empty fluid reservoir
2 Broken hydraulic pipe line
3 Ruptured master cylinder seal
4 Ruptured wheel cylinder or caliper seal

(f) Reservoir empties too quickly

1 Leaks in pipe lines
2 Deteriorated cylinder seals

(g) Pedal yields under continuous pressure

1 Faulty master cylinder seals
2 Faulty wheel cylinder or caliper seals
3 Leak in brake pipe or hose

CHAPTER 11

THE ELECTRICAL SYSTEM

11:1 Description

All models covered by this manual have 12-volt electrical systems in which the negative terminal of the battery is earthed to the car bodywork.

There are wiring diagrams in **Technical Data** at the end of this manual which will enable those with electrical experience to trace and correct faults.

Instructions for servicing the items of electrical equipment are given in this chapter, but it must be pointed out that it is not sensible to try to repair units which are seriously defective, electrically or mechanically. Such faulty equipment should be replaced by new or reconditioned units which can be obtained on an exchange basis.

11:2 The battery

To maintain the performance of the battery, it is essential to carry out the following operations, particularly in winter when heavy current demands must be met.

Keep the top and surrounding parts of the battery dry and clean, as dampness can cause current leakage. Clean off corrosion from the metal parts of the battery mounting with diluted ammonia and coat them with anti-sulphuric paint. Clean the terminal posts and smear them with petroleum jelly, tightening the terminal clamp securely. High electrical resistance due to corrosion at the battery terminals can be responsible for a lack of sufficient current to operate the starter motor.

Regularly remove the cover from the battery and check the electrolyte level in each cell, topping up with distilled water if necessary to just cover the separators.

If a battery fault is suspected, test the condition of the cells with a hydrometer. **Never add neat acid to the battery. If it is necessary to prepare new electrolyte due to loss or spillage, add sulphuric acid to distilled water. It is highly dangerous to add water to acid.** It is safest to have the battery refilled with electrolyte if it is necessary by a service station.

The indications from the hydrometer readings of the specific gravity are as follows:

	Specific gravity
For climates below 27°C or 80°F	
Cell fully charged	1.270 to 1.290
Cell half discharged	1.190 to 1.210
Cell discharged	1.110 to 1.130
For climates above 27°C or 80°F	
Cell fully charged	1.210 to 1.230
Cell half discharged	1.130 to 1.150
Cell discharged	1.050 to 1.070

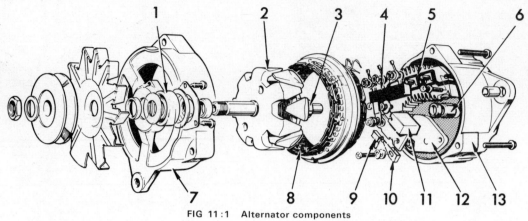

FIG 11 :1   Alternator components

Key to Fig 11 :1   1 Drive end bearing   2 Rotor   3 Slip rings   4 Diode trio   5 Rectifier   6 Slip ring end bearing
7 Drive end bracket   8 Stator   9 Brush   10 Brush lead clip   11 Brush holder   12 Regulator   13 Slip ring end bracket

These figures assume an electrolyte temperature of 60°F or 16°C. If the temperature of the electrolyte exceeds this, add .002 to the readings for each 5°F or 3°C rise. Subtract .002 for any corresponding drop below 60°F or 16°C.

All cells should read approximately the same. If one differs radically from the others, it may be due to an internal fault, or to spillage or leakage of the electrolyte.

If the battery is in a low state of charge take the car for a long daylight run or put the battery on a charger at 5 amps with the filler caps removed until it gases freely. Do not use a naked light near the battery as the gas is inflammable. If the battery is to stand unused for long periods, give a refreshing charge every month. It will be ruined if it is left uncharged.

11 :3 The alternator

The alternator provides current for the various items of electrical equipment and to charge the battery, the unit operating at all engine speeds. The current produced is alternate, this being rectified to direct current supply by diodes mounted in the alternator casing. Alternator drive is taken from the fan belt. Very little maintenance is needed, apart from the occasional check on belt tension as described in **Chapter 4, Section 4 :4** and on the condition and tightness of the wiring connections.

The alternator must never be run with the battery disconnected, nor must the battery cables be reversed at any time. Test connections must be carefully made, and the battery and alternator must be completely disconnected before any electric welding is carried out on

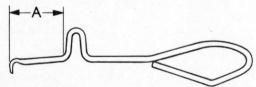

FIG 11 :2   Details of tool for earthing alternator field brush clip. A = 25mm (1in)

any part of the car. The engine must never be started with a battery charger still connected to the battery. These warnings must be observed, otherwise extensive damage to the alternator components, particularly diodes, will result.

The alternator is designed and constructed to give many years of trouble-free service. If, however, a fault should develop in the unit, it should be checked and serviced by a fully equipped service station or a reconditioned unit obtained and fitted. **FIG 11 :1** shows the components of the Delco-Remy DN.460 alternator which is fitted to all models.

Alternator testing :

A simple check on alternator charging can be carried out after dark by switch on the headlamps and starting the engine. If the alternator is charging, the headlamps will brighten considerably as the system voltage rises from the nominal battery voltage to the higher figure produced by the alternator. A more accurate check is to earth the field brush clip while the alternator is operating and measure the current being generated. The brush clip is earthed by using a tool (see **FIG 11 :2**) inserted into the hole in the drive end bracket (see **FIG 11 :3**), the loop acting as a stop to prevent the end fouling the rotor. Connect a suitable ammeter into the positive lead between the alternator and the battery and run the engine at approximately 3000rev/min when a current of 35amps should be indicated.

If the alternator is not charging, or if the correct maximum output reading cannot be obtained by the method described, check the wiring and connections in the charging circuit. If these are in order, the alternator unit is at fault and must be checked and repaired by a service station.

Alternator removal :

Disconnect the battery, then disconnect the cables to the alternator. Slacken the alternator mounting bolts, swing the unit towards the engine to slacken the drive belt, then remove the belt. Unbolt and remove the alternator.

Refitting is a reversal of the removal procedure, adjusting the belt tension as described in **Chapter 4, Section 4:4**. Note also the warning given in that chapter concerning the correct tightening of the alternator mounting bolts.

11:4 Testing starter motor

The starter motor tests given in this section apply to either type of starter motor as described in **Sections 11:5** or **11:6**. The tests are carried out with the starter motor fitted in the vehicle.

When the starter switch (ignition key) is turned fully to the right a small current operates a solenoid and closes its contacts. These contacts which are capable of handling a heavy current, connect the battery direct to the starter by heavy cables. An additional contact on the solenoid feeds current to the ignition coil, without passing through the resistor, to provide a more powerful ignition current when starting (see **Chapter 3**).

When checking starter troubles, first ensure that the battery is in good condition and that all battery and starter connections are in good order. A corroded battery terminal or bad earth connection may have sufficient electrical resistance to make the starter inoperative, though it may pass enough current for lamps and accessories.

To check the solenoid, operate the starter switch, when a click should be heard from the solenoid indicating that the contact bridge is moving. If no click can be heard, carry out the following tests using a 0 to 20 range voltmeter.

Check the supply to the solenoid by connecting voltmeter positive to white/red terminal and voltmeter negative to earth (see **FIG 11:4**). When the starter switch is operated the voltmeter should record battery voltage. No reading indicates a faulty starter switch or wiring.

Closure of the solenoid switch contacts can be checked by connecting the voltmeter across the main switch terminals (see **FIG 11:5**). Operate the starter switch and, if the contacts are closing correctly, the voltmeter reading should drop to zero. If the reading does not drop to zero, the solenoid switch is faulty and must be renewed.

On models fitted with a 5M90/PE starter motor, connect the voltmeter as shown in **FIG 11:6** to check the voltage across the main starter solenoid terminals. A reading of 12 volts should be obtained. Operate the starter switch and, if the solenoid contacts are closing, the voltmeter reading will drop to zero. If the reading fails to drop to zero, the solenoid on the starter must be renewed.

11:5 Starter motor M35J/1

The M35J/1 starter is a series-wound four pole unit incorporating an inertia-operated pinion which auto-matically engages the flywheel ring gear upon operation and disengages when the engine starts. A face-type moulded commutator is provided together with a fully insulated plastic brush box which is riveted to the commutator end bracket. The wedge-shaped brushes are

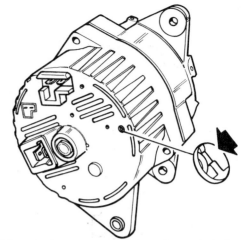

FIG 11:3 Insert the tool through the hole in the drive end bracket to earth the clip

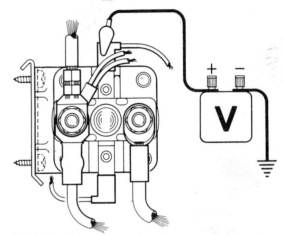

FIG 11:4 Voltmeter connections to check starter switch and wiring

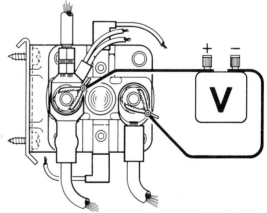

FIG 11:5 Voltmeter connections to check solenoid switch contacts

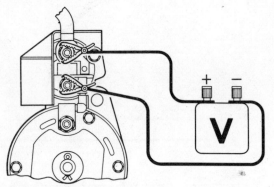

FIG 11:6 Voltmeter connections to check current supply to 5M90/PE starter

provided with a keyway to ensure correct location and the brush springs are held captive in the brush box. **FIG 11:7** shows a cutaway view of the starter motor.

Removal:

In order to remove the starter it is necessary to first remove the righthand engine mounting. Remove the air cleaner, then raise the front of the vehicle and support it safely on stands. Support the front of the engine and remove the nut securing the bracket to the righthand engine mounting. Raise the front of the engine, remove the three bolts from the engine mounting then withdraw the mounting bracket. Remove the mounting and impact cup using special tool VR2217.

Disconnect the feed wire and remove the starter securing bolts. Withdraw the starter from underneath the alternator.

Dismantling:

If the starter drive is in good condition it need not be dismantled but should be washed in petrol. Oil must not be used as this will collect grit and cause the starter to fail to engage. If the drive has to be dismantled either for servicing or for removal of drive end bracket, proceed as follows:

Compress the thrust spring. This operation is facilitated if the special spring compressor JWP376 is used. Remove the circlip from the end of the shaft and release the spring. Remove the spring collar, spring and thrust washer. Withdraw the pinion assembly and screwed sleeve from the armature shaft. If necessary, rotate the pinion slightly so as to line up the splined washer inside the pinion barrel with the splines on the shaft. The thrust spring can be checked by comparison with a new spring.

Detach the commutator end bracket from the body, making sure that the thrust washer which is arrowed in **FIG 11:8** is not lost. With the pinion assembly removed as described previously, remove the two bolts and detach the drive end bracket and armature assembly (see **FIG 11:9**). Remove the armature shaft bushes if they are worn or damaged. The bush in the commutator end bracket can be driven out with a punch.

Servicing:

Check the thickness of the four brushes. If any brush is worn to a length of 9.5mm (0.38in) or less, all four brushes should be renewed. The commutator end bracket brushes are supplied complete with new terminal as shown in **FIG 11:10**, in a kit which also includes two field brushes. Field brushes can be renewed without removing the field coils from the yoke. Cut off the original brush leads 8mm (0.30in) from the aluminium tag. Make sure that the new leads are located correctly for length, then solder in position (see **FIG 11:11**).

If brush springs are weak or otherwise unserviceable, the commutator end bracket assembly must be renewed as the springs are not serviced separately.

The face of the commutator should be cleaned with a with a petrol moistened cloth while rotating the armature. Do not saturate as petrol is harmful to the windings. If the commutator will not clean up properly by this means, it can be polished by the careful use of fine glass paper. To remove deep burning or pitting, the commutator can be skimmed while the armature is rotated in a lathe, provided that dimension A in **FIG 11:12** is not reduced below 2mm (0.08in). The insulators must not be undercut and the commutator must be finally polished with very fine glass paper.

Field coils can be checked for insulation after detaching the earthed end of the winding from the yoke. When installing field coils, position the pole shoes so that the threaded hole in the end of one of the shoes is adjacent to the field winding earth joint, with another threaded hole diametrically opposite (see **FIG 11:13**).

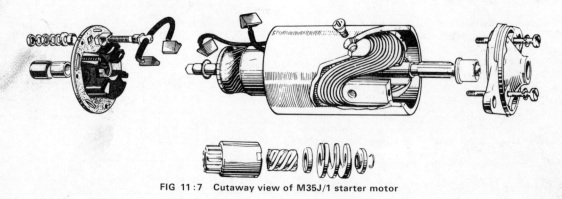

FIG 11:7 Cutaway view of M35J/1 starter motor

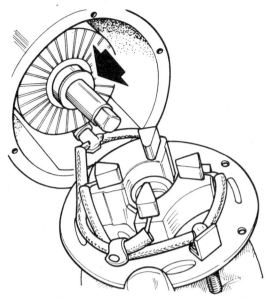

FIG 11:8 The commutator end bracket and thrust washer (arrowed)

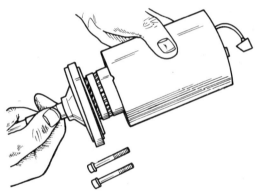

FIG 11:9 Removing drive end bracket and armature

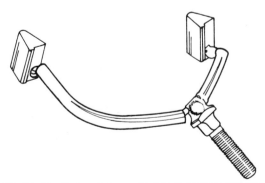

FIG 11:10 Commutator end bracket brushes and terminal

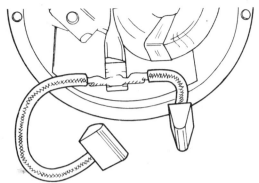

FIG 11:11 New field brushes soldered to existing lead ends

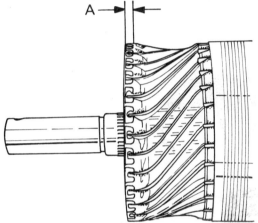

FIG 11:12 Minimum thickness of commutator at A must not be less than 2mm (0.08in)

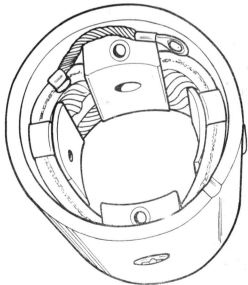

FIG 11:13 Field coil installation

CHEVETTE

FIG 11:14 Forcing lubricant through an armature shaft bush

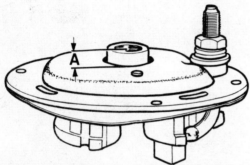

FIG 11:15 Press in new commutator end bracket bush so that dimension A is 5.5mm (0.22in)

Ensure that the insulator is positioned between the brush connection and yoke before tightening the pole screws.

If new bushes are to be installed they must first be properly lubricated. Place a forefinger over one end and fill the bush with engine oil. Place the thumb over the other end and apply pressure until oil seeps through the bush wall (see FIG 11:14). The bush in the commutator end bracket must be pressed in so that dimension A in FIG 11:15 is 5.5mm (0.22in).

Reassembly:

Reassembly is a reversal of the dismantling procedure. Make sure that the thrust washer is installed on the armature shaft before assembly the commutator end bracket to the yoke (see FIG 11:8).

Refitting:

Refitting is a reversal of the removal procedure. After installing the starter, reassemble the engine mounting and impact cup then tighten the mounting to 29lb ft. The engine mounting bracket to crankcase attaching bolts must be thoroughly cleaned and smeared with Loctite 270 (AVV) before installation to prevent the bolts from working loose (see also Chapter 1).

11:6 Starter motor 5M90/PE

The 5M90/PE starter is a brush-type series wound motor equipped with an overrunning clutch and operated by a solenoid. The armature shaft is supported in metal bushes. A face-type moulded commutator and fully insulated plastic brush box is provided. The wedge-shaped brushes are provided with a keyway to ensure correct location and the brush springs are held captive in the brush box. Apart from the pre-engagement mechanism, the unit is very similar internally to the M35J/1 starter described in Section 11:5, it being fitted as an optional heavy-duty alternative on some models.

When the starter is operated from the switch, the engagement lever moves the pinion into mesh with the engine ring gear. When the pinion meshes with the ring

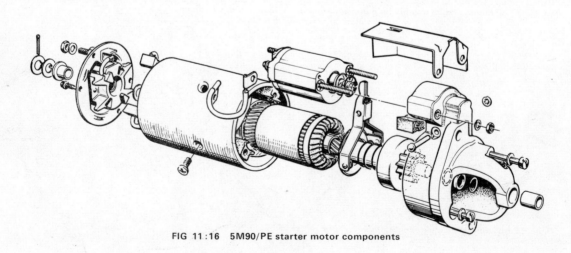

FIG 11:16   5M90/PE starter motor components

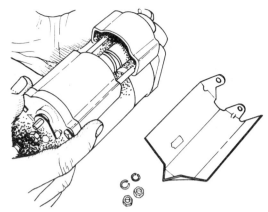

FIG 11:17   Solenoid removal

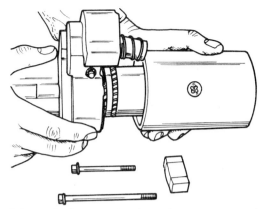

FIG 11:18   Drive end bracket and armature removal

gear teeth, the solenoid contact closes the circuit and the starter motor operates to turn the engine. When the engine starts, the speed of the rotating ring gear causes the pinion to overrun the clutch and armature. The pinion continues in engagement until the switch is released when the engagement lever returns it to the rest position under spring action.

Removal:

Follow the removal procedure given in **Section 11:5**, noting that the securing bolts on the 5M90/PE starter are socket-headed and a $\frac{5}{16}$in hexagon bit adaptor and extension bar are required when removing and installing the bolts.

Dismantling:

FIG 11:16 shows the starter motor components.

Detach the connecting link, remove the two securing nuts and heat shield then detach the solenoid (see **FIG 11:17**). Detach the commutator end bracket from the yoke making sure that the thrust washer, arrowed in **FIG 11:8** is not lost. Remove the two bolts and detach the drive end bracket complete with armature as shown in **FIG 11:18**.

Drive out the engagement lever pin through the retaining ring as shown in **FIG 11:19**, then remove the armature from the drive end bracket. The drive pinion assembly can be removed from the armature shaft as shown in **FIG 11:20**. Tap down the thrust collar 1 with a suitable tube then remove the circlip 2.

Servicing:

Servicing of the brush gear and springs, commutator, field coils and armature shaft bushes is carried out in the manner described for M35J/1 units in **Section 11:5**. The drive end bracket bush should be pressed in until it is flush with the bracket. The commutator end bracket bush should be pressed in until its shoulder contacts the bracket.

Check the drive pinion assembly for wear or damage. Turn the pinion on the shaft in each direction to check the roller clutch. A clutch in good condition will provide instantaneous take-up of drive in one direction and

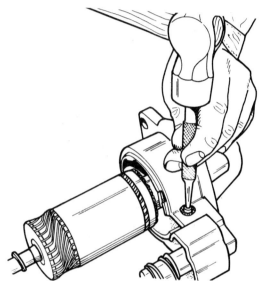

FIG 11:19   Engagement lever pin removal

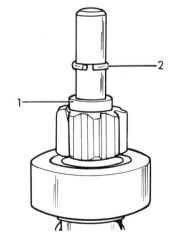

FIG 11:20   Drive pinion thrust collar 1 and circlip 2

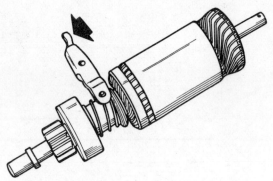

FIG 11:21 Radiused edge of engagement lever must be towards armature

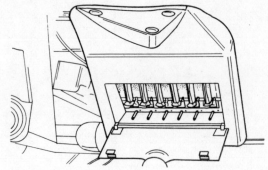

FIG 11:24 The fusebox is fitted with pull-down cover

rotate smoothly and easily in the other. The pinion assembly should move freely round and along the armature shaft splines without roughness or binding. If any part is damaged or faulty, the pinion assembly must be renewed as no component is serviced separately.

Reassembly:

Reassembly is a reversal of the removal procedure, noting the following points:

When reassembling the drive pinion to the armature make sure that the radiused edge of the lever (arrowed in **FIG 11:21**) is towards the armature. After reassembling the armature and drive assembly to the drive end bracket, secure the engagement lever pin with a new retaining ring. Make sure that the thrust washer is installed on the armature shaft before refitting the commutator end bracket to the yoke.

Adjust the armature shaft end float, referring to **FIG 11:22**. Fit thrust plate 1 and temporarily install the splitpin and use feeler gauges to check that end float is no more than 0.25mm (0.010in). If this figure is exceeded, adjust by varying the number of shims 2 between the thrust plate and splitpin. When correct, fit and lock the splitpin.

Lubricate the slot and retaining plate on the solenoid plunger with recommended grease before assembling to the engagement lever.

Fit the rubber grommet between the drive end bracket and yoke as shown in **FIG 11:23** before installing the solenoid and heat shield.

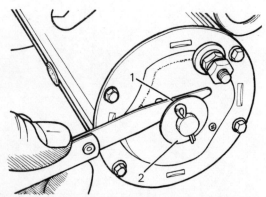

FIG 11:22 Checking armature end float between thrust plate 1 and shim 2

Refitting:

Refitting is a reversal of the removal procedure. After installing the starter, reassemble the engine mounting and impact cup and tighten the mounting to 29lb ft, using tool VR2217. The engine mounting bracket to crankcase attaching bolts must be thoroughly cleaned and smeared with Loctite 270(AVV) to prevent the bolts from working loose.

11:7 Fuses

The main wiring circuits are protected by conventional fuses and, additionally, by means of two fusible links.

Six 16 amp fuses are contained in the fuse box which is clipped into a bracket secured to the bottom of the instrument panel outboard of the steering column (see **FIG 11:24**). The fuses are numbered 1 to 6 and the

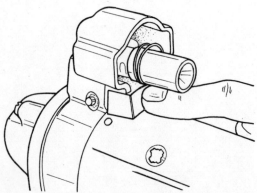

FIG 11:23 Installing rubber grommet

numbers are located behind each fuse. Number 1 is at the lefthand end. The circuits protected by the fuses are as follows:

1 Righthand side and tail lamps, instrument lamps and, if fitted, cigar lighter bulb, fog lamps and fog rear guard lamps.

2 Lefthand side and tail lamps, number plate lamp and, if fitted, engine compartment lamp.

3 Interior lamp, horn, headlamp flasher and, if fitted, hazard warning system and clock.

4 Tailgate heated window and reversing lamps.

5 Stop lamps, turn signal and warning lamps, oil and alternator warning lamps, voltage stabiliser, fuel and temperature gauges, heater motor and brake pressure warning system.

6 Windscreen wiper and washer and, if fitted, headlamp wash/wipe, radio and cigar lighter element.

If a fuse blows, it may be due to a temporary overload in which case the fitting of a new fuse will be all that is required. However, if a new fuse blows immediately the faulty component must be located and repaired.

The two fusible links are connected into the main battery feed at the starter solenoid switch which is mounted on a bracket adjacent to the battery. The links are designed to burn out in the event of a heavy overload due to a shortcircuit or similar fault, in order to protect the entire electrical system with the exception of the starter. One of the links protects the lighting switch and the feed to No. 1 and 2 fuses, the other link protects the starter switch and ignition system and the feeds to Nos. 3, 4, 5 and 6 fuses.

If a fusible link burns out, the cause of the overload must be traced and rectified before a new link is fitted. Fusible link renewal is carried out using a repair kit.

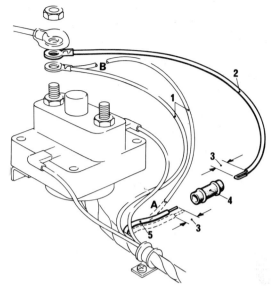

FIG 11:25   Fusible link renewal

Key to Fig 11:25   1 Original fusible links   2 Replacement fusible link   3 Measurement of approximately 12mm (0.5in)   4 Butt connector   5 Two brown cables or single brown/blue cable (part of existing harness)

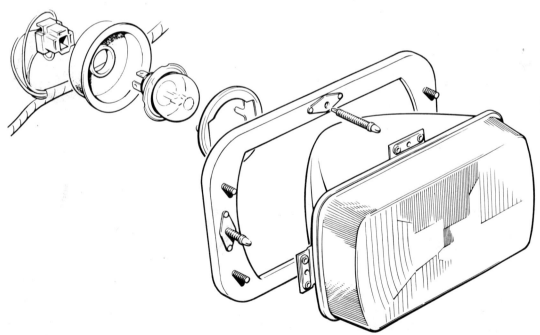

FIG 11:26   Cibie headlamp components

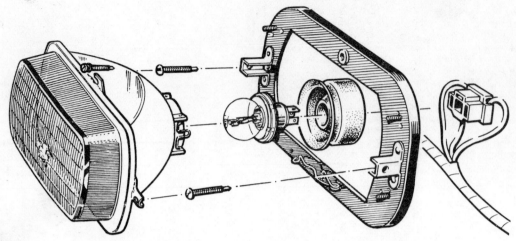

FIG 11:27 Lucas headlamp components

Refer to **FIG 11:25**. Cut away the damaged fusible link from junction on harness at point A and at ring terminal point B. Strip approximately 20mm (0.80in) of insulation from the fusible link and double back the wire. Strip approximately 12mm (0.50in) of insulation from the harness cable(s). Insert the main harness and fusible link wire into butt connector and crimp to secure. Assemble the fusible link ring terminal to the solenoid switch terminal.

11:8 Lamps

Headlamps:

Lamps of either Cibie or Lucas manufacture may be fitted, as shown in **FIG 11:26** or **11:27**. The unit houses a twin-filament bulb for main and dipped beams.

Access to the headlamp bulb is from inside the engine compartment where a rubber cover must be pulled back to expose the securing spring clip.

The removal of a complete light unit entails removal of the headlamp surround which is secured by three screws. The Cibie light unit is removed by easing it off the beam trim screws. Do not disturb the trim screws or the lamp aim will be altered. To remove the Lucas unit, release the retaining spring at the bottom of the lamp then ease the bracket out of the top beam trim screw. Do not disturb the trim screws.

The headlamp assembly complete with light unit can be removed after detaching the wiring connector and removing the four securing nuts.

Beam setting:

This work is best carried out by a service station having special optical equipment, in order to achieve accurate results. When the work is carried out, the car must be normally loaded and the headlamps switched to dipped beam.

Headlamp wash/wipe:

The headlamp wash/wipe system is available in certain export territories as an optional extra. The wash jets are fed by an electric pump from the reservoir mounted on the lefthand wheelhouse panel. To prevent fluid drainage when the system is not in use a valve is provided in the tube inside the reservoir and a second valve is fitted in the tube from the pump to the jets. The blade for each headlamp is powered by an individual electric motor mounted on the front panel, the blade arm being attached directly to the motor shaft. The motors are sealed units incorporating self-parking switches. The wash jets are attached to the wiper arms and to allow flexibility in operation, the wash tube is wound twice around the motor spindle. Electrical power for the system is taken from No. 6 fuse via a line fuse and is controlled by the combined windshield and headlamp wash/wipe switch on the steering column. The system is operated when the ignition is switched on by depressing the knob on the switch lever. Additionally, the system can also be operated simultaneously with the windscreen wash by moving the switch lever upwards towards the steering wheel. Electrical power for the motors is fed via a relay mounted on the lefthand wheelhouse panel, a line fuse being incorporated.

To gain access for removing blades and/or arms, the headlamp surrounds must be removed after detaching the three screws. The blade can be unclipped from the arm and the arm can be withdrawn from the motor shaft after detaching the tube from the jet and removing the nut from the shaft. When fitting an arm, make sure that the motor is in the parked position and locate the arm so that the blade is adjacent to the outer edge of the lamp lens. A wash/wipe motor can be removed after detaching the blade and arm and disconnecting the wires at the plug and socket connector. Remove the two nuts and withdraw the motor from the front panel. To gain access to the motor on the lefthand lamp, the reservoir must first be withdrawn.

Front parking and turn signal lamps:

Access to the bulbs in these lamps can be gained after removing the two screws and detaching the plastic lens cover.

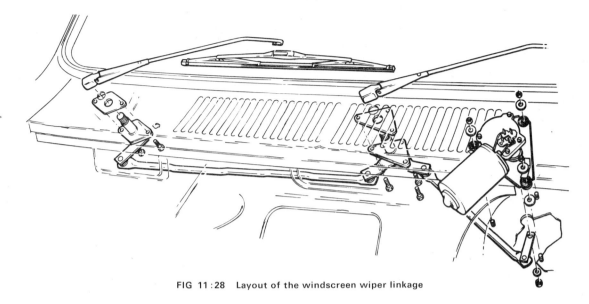

FIG 11:28   Layout of the windscreen wiper linkage

Rear lamps:

Access to the bulbs in these lamps is gained by removing the plastic lens cover which is retained by two screws. The stop/tail lamp bulb is of the dual filament type.

Number plate lamp:

To gain access to the bulb, remove the two screws and ease the front of the lens down to disengage the rear end from the body. Pull the bulb holder out of the clips and detach the wedge base capless bulb.

Interior lamp:

To gain access to the bulb, ease the lamp over to the righthand side on righthand drive models or to the lefthand side on lefthand drive models, then withdraw the unit from the roof interior.

11:9 Windscreen wipers and washers

Wipers:

The windscreen wipers are operated by a two-speed electric motor incorporating a self-parking switch. The motor is fitted to a mounting bracket which is rubber mounted on three studs in the dash panel. The two wiper pivot housings are bolted to the dash panel and the pivot cranks are connected to the motor by long and short rods and a crank. The layout of the system is shown in **FIG 11:28**. Note that a slightly different linkage layout is employed on lefthand drive models.

To remove the wiper motor, first remove the parcel shelf then remove the nuts and withdraw the crank from the motor cross shaft. Disconnect the wiring plug from the motor, remove the three nuts from the mounting studs and withdraw the motor and bracket. When refitting the motor, ensure that the key in the crank engages keyway in the cross shaft. It is recommended that a faulty motor should be taken to a service station for attention or replacement and not dismantled by the owner.

To gain the necessary access for wiper linkage removal, it is necessary to remove the instrument panel cover. The steering wheel and column canopy, demist tube on righthand drive models, instrument assembly, lighting switch and parcel shelf must be removed first. The instrument panel cover is retained by two nuts and six clips. Remove the nuts and pull the cover away. Lever the wiper arms and blades from the wiper pivots. Remove the nut and ease the crank off the wiper motor cross shaft. Remove the bolt securing the pivots and withdraw the wiper linkage. When refitting the linkage, ensure that the key in the motor crank engages the slot in the motor cross shaft.

11:10 Instrument panel

The instrument panel is secured to a hood by two screws and the assembly is retained in the facia panel by two spring clips and four tabs.

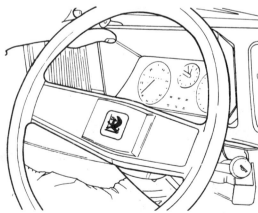

FIG 11:29   Instrument panel removal

Removal:

The bayonet-type speedometer cable connector can be detached from the rear of the speedometer by gaining access beneath the instrument panel. On righthand drive models remove the windshield demist duct first. Release the instrument panel assembly from the clips by reaching behind the unit and pushing it towards the steering wheel, as shown in **FIG 11 : 29**. Refit the instrument panel in the reverse order of removal.

11 : 11 Fault diagnosis

(a) Battery discharged

1 Terminal connections loose or dirty
2 Shorts in lighting circuits
3 Alternator not charging
4 Regulator faulty
5 Battery internally defective

(b) Insufficient charge rate

1 Check 1 and 4 in (a)
2 Drive belt slipping
3 Alternator defective

(c) Battery will not hold charge

1 Low electrolyte level
2 Battery plates sulphated
3 Electrolyte leakage from cracked case
4 Battery plate separators defective

(d) Battery overcharged

1 Regulator faulty

(e) Alternator output low or nil

1 Drive belt broken or slipping
2 Regulator faulty
3 Brushes sticking, springs weak or broken
4 Faulty internal windings
5 Defective diode(s)

(f) Starter motor lacks power or will not turn

1 Battery discharged, loose cable connections
2 Starter switch or solenoid faulty
3 Brushes worn or sticking, leads detached or shorting
4 Commutator dirty or worn
5 Starter shaft bent
6 Engine abnormally stiff

(g) Starter runs but does not turn engine

1 Pinion engagement mechanism faulty
2 Broken teeth on pinion or engine ring gear

(h) Starter motor rough or noisy

1 Mounting bolts loose
2 Pinion engagement mechanism faulty
3 Damaged pinion or engine ring gear teeth

(j) Noisy starter when engine is running

1 Pinion return mechanism faulty
2 Mounting bolts loose

(k) Starter motor inoperative

1 Check 1 and 3 in (f)
2 Armature or field coils faulty

(l) Lamps inoperative or erratic

1 Battery low, bulbs burned out
2 Faulty earthing of lamps or battery
3 Lighting switch faulty, loose or broken connections

(m) Wiper motor sluggish, taking high current

1 Wiper motor internally defective
2 Linkage worn or binding

CHAPTER 12

THE BODYWORK

12:1 Bodywork finish

Large scale repairs to body panels are best left to expert panel beaters. Even small dents can be tricky, as too much hammering will stretch the metal and make things worse instead of better. If panel beating is to be attempted, use a dolly on the opposite side of the panel. The head of a large hammer will suffice for small dents, but for large dents, a block of metal will be necessary. Use light hammer blows to reshape the panel, pressing the dolly against the opposite side of the panel to absorb the blows. If this method is used to reduce the depth of dents, final smoothing with a suitable filler will be easier, although it may be better to avoid hammering minor dents and just use the filler.

Clean the area to be filled, making sure that it is free from paint, rust and grease, then roughen the area with emerycloth to ensure a good bond. Use a proprietary Fibreglass filler paste mixed according to the manufacturer's instructions and press it into the dent with a putty knife or similar flat-bladed tool. Allow the filler to stand proud of the surrounding area to allow for rubbing down after hardening. Use a file and emerycloth or a disc sander to blend the repaired area to the surrounding bodywork, using finer grade abrasive as the work nears completion. Apply a coat of primer surfacer and, when it is dry, rub down with 'Wet or Dry' paper lubricated with soapy water, finishing with 400 grade. Apply more primer and repeat the operation until the surface is perfectly smooth. Take time on achieving the best finish possible at this stage as it will control the final effect.

The touching-up of paintwork can be carried out with self-spraying cans of paint, these being available in a wide range of colours. Use a piece of newspaper or board as a test panel to practise on first, so that the action of the spray will be familiar when it is used on the panel. Before spraying the panel, remove all traces of wax polish. Mask off large areas such as windows with newspaper and masking tape. Small areas such as trim strips or door handles can be wrapped with masking tape or carefully coated with grease or Vaseline. Apply the touching-up paint, spraying with short bursts and keeping the spray moving. Do not attempt to cover the area in one coat, applying several coats with a few minutes' drying time between each. If too much paint is applied at one time, runs may develop. If so, do not try to remove the run by wiping but wait until it is dry and rub down as before.

After the final coat has been applied, allow a few hours of drying time before blending the new finish to the old with fine cutting compound, buffing with a light, circular motion. Finish with the application of a good quality polish.

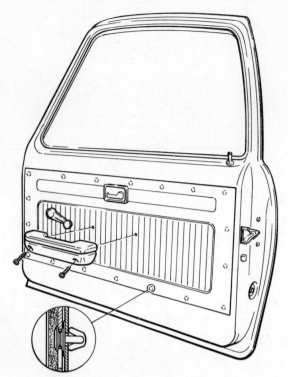

FIG 12:1   Door trim pad attachments

12:2 Door components

Removal of the complete door assembly from the car bodywork requires the use of special tools to extract the split hinge pins, so this work is best left to a service station. However, removal and servicing of door components can be carried out without the need for door removal as described in this section.

Trim pad removal:

Take out the two screws and detach the armrest (see **FIG 12:1**). Use a thin blade to prise off the remote control handle escutcheon, which is retained by pegs which clip into holes in the remote control casing. Use a suitable tool such as D1021 or similar to press the spring retainer from the groove in the window regulator handle boss (see **FIG 12:2**). Remove the regulator handle.

Use a thin bladed tool fitted between the trim pad and door panel to lever the spring clips from position and release the pad. To prevent damage to the pad, make sure that the tool is positioned as close as possible to each fastener as it is levered from position.

If access to door internal components is required, the plastic water deflector sheet must be removed from the door inner panel.

Refit the trim pad in the reverse order of removal. To install the water deflector, apply recommended adhesive to edges of deflector and mating surfaces of door inner panel, allow the adhesive to become tacky, then press the deflector into place carefully smoothing out wrinkles. If a good seal is not obtained, water may enter and saturate the trim pad. When installing the trim pad, refer to **FIG 12:3** and make sure that spring 3 is located around the window regulator spindle and between the trim pad 1 and door inner panel 2. The large conical end of the spring must be against the trim pad.

Door locks:

For access to door lock components, first remove the trim pad as described previously. The remote control mechanism is attached to the door inner panel by two screws and connected to the lock by a rod, as shown in **FIG 12:4**. The slotted mounting holes in the mechanism allow it to be moved for adjustment of the control linkage. Before finally tightening the attaching screws, move the control assembly forward to eliminate free movement in the linkage without applying any load on the locking mechanism. Lubricate the friction surfaces of the control and rod with high melting point grease.

The door lock and catch are operated by a series of rods, as shown in **FIG 12:5**. The internal lock batten is screwed onto the upper end of rod 1, the remote control rod 4 operating the catch release from inside the car. The outside handle is connected to the catch release by rod 2, rod 3 operating the locking mechanism from the outside key lock.

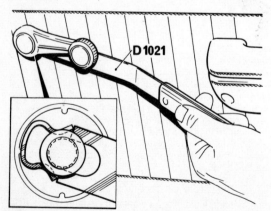

FIG 12:2   Removing the regulator handle spring retainer

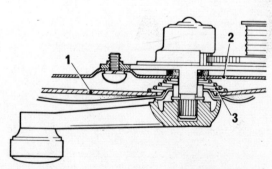

FIG 12:3   Regulator handle installation

Key to Fig 12:3   1 Trim pad   2 Door inner panel
3 Spring

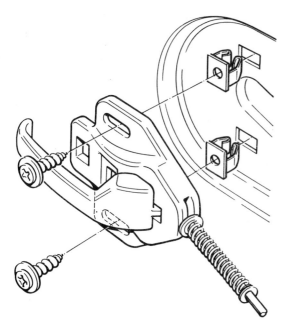

FIG 12:4   Door lock remote control mechanism

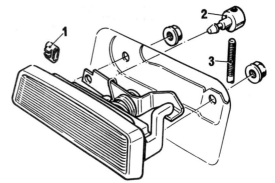

FIG 12:6   Door outside handle assembly

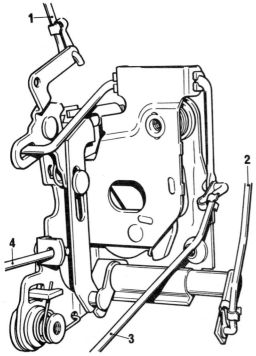

FIG 12:5   Door lock components

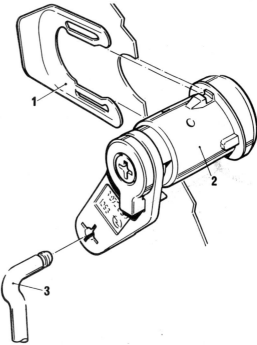

FIG 12:7   Outside key lock components

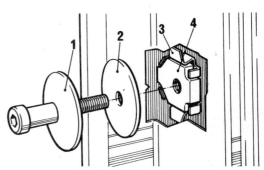

FIG 12:8   Door lock striker

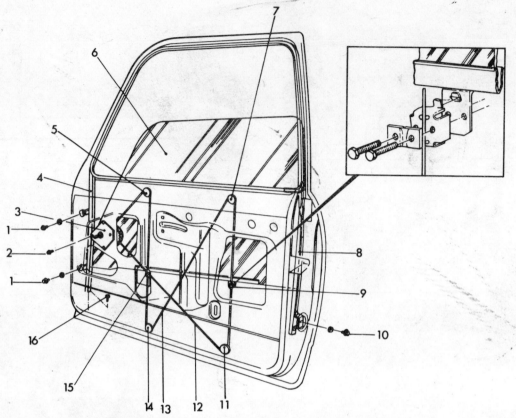

FIG 12:9   Door window glass and regulator mechanism layout

Key to Fig 12:9   1 Glass front run channel lower bolts   2 Regulator attachment screw   3 Regulator   4 Glass front run channel   5 Front upper roller   6 Window glass   7 Rear upper roller   8 Glass rear run channel   9 Cable clamp   10 Bolt   11 Rear lower roller   12 Inner cable   13 Outer cable   14 Front lower roller   15 Cable clamp   16 Bolt

To remove the lock assembly, first remove the trim pad as described previously. The door window glass must be raised fully. Refer to **FIG 12:6** and remove the nuts securing the outside handle then prise the adjusting nut 2 from the clip 1. Remove the outside handle from the door panel. Refer to **FIG 12:7** and remove the clip 1 from the outside key lock, gaining access through the aperture in the door inner panel. Prise the rod 3 from the lock lever and detach the key lock assembly.

Remove the glass rear run channel as described later, after which the lock assembly can be detached from the door inner panel.

Refit the door lock assembly in the reverse order of removal. Friction surfaces of lock and rods should be smeared with high melting point grease before installing the lock in the door. When fitting the lock barrel to the key lock, lubricate with dry graphite. Do not use ordinary oil which could result in damage to locks caused by grit or fluff adhering to the components. When installing the outside handle, refer to **FIG 12:6** and adjust the nut 2 on the release rod 3 so that free movement is eliminated without applying a load on the locking mechanism and handle.

Door lock striker:

The door lock striker components are shown in **FIG 12:8**. The anchor plate 4 is held to the door lock pillar by a bracket 3. Sufficient movement of the plate is provided to permit sideways and up and down adjustment of the striker. Fore and aft adjustment of the striker 1 is obtained by packing washers 2. A special hexagon key will be needed to remove or tighten the striker bolt. The point of contact of the door lock fork bolt on the striker can be determined by pressing plasticine onto the waisted portion of the striker. Close and open the door and check the indentation made in the plasticine. The contact point should be approximately in the centre of the striker. If not, adjust by fitting packing washers of different thickness. When installing the striker, tighten to 40lb ft.

Window glass and regulator removal:

The door window glass is raised and lowered by a continuous cable which runs on four roller guides and is operated by a grooved drum regulator (see **FIG 12:9**). The glass support channel is attached to the cable by two clamps.

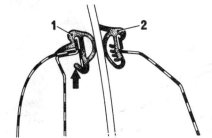

FIG 12:10 Door waist inner 1 and outer 2 weather strips

Remove the trim pad as described previously, then lower the window until the clamp bolts are aligned with the apertures in the inner door panel. Slacken the bolts to release the clamps. Remove the two bolts shown in **FIG 12:9** which secure the glass front run channel. Slacken but do not remove the upper bolt for this channel, which is located at the front edge of the door panel just above the bottom of the glass aperture. Lower the glass to the bottom of the door.

Prise away the door waist inner 1 and outer 2 weather strips shown in **FIG 12:10**. On reassembly, the inner weather strip must be installed first ensuring that the bottom lip (arrowed) is correctly located over the flange.

Raise the glass and withdraw through the inside of the door upper frame. Slacken the bolt securing the adjustable rear lower pulley (11 in **FIG 12:9**) to slacken the cable. Remove the three securing screws and detach the regulator assembly from the door panel. Regulators are handed and identified by the letter R or L, for righthand or lefthand, situated on the inside face of the drum.

Refitting:

Install the regulator to the door inner panel making sure that the rubber sealing ring is located between the panel and regulator spindle. Refer to **FIG 12:9**. Position the regulator drum so that the inner cable 12 is pointing towards the rear lower adjustable roller 14 and wrap the inner cable around the roller. Maintaining tension on the cable, wind the cable onto the drum by rotating the regulator handle anticlockwise on righthand door, clockwise on lefthand door until four grooves on the drum are full of cable and the outer cable is vertical (see **FIG 12:11**). Keep the outer cable clear of the drum while winding the inner cable, so that the outer cable does not wrap itself around the drum. Wrap the cable around the rear upper roller 7, then around the front lower roller 14 and finally around front upper roller 5, making sure that the cable does not become kinked. Tension the cable by applying firm hand pressure on the adjustable roller 14 and firmly tighten the securing bolt.

From the position shown in **FIG 12:11**, rotate the window regulator handle clockwise on righthand door or anticlockwise on lefthand door until the indicator mark on regulator drum (arrowed in **FIG 12:12**), appears through the hole in the door inner panel for the second time.

Make sure that the support channel is located on the window glass as shown in **FIG 12:13**, with dimension A

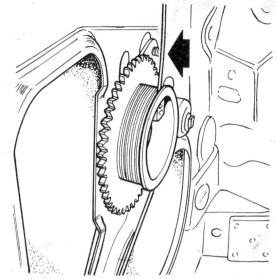

FIG 12:11 Inner cable wound four turns around regulator drum with outer cable (arrowed) vertical

FIG 12:12 Indicator mark on regulator drum

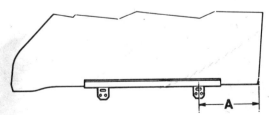

FIG 12:13 Align glass support channel so that dimension A is 235.5mm (9.26in) for two-door models or 168.3mm (6.60in) on four-door models

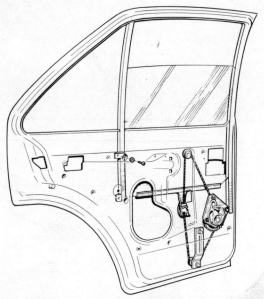

FIG 12:14   Rear door glass and regulator mechanism

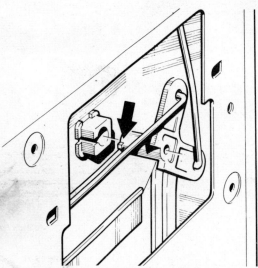

FIG 12:15   Rear door lock interior operation. Arrow indicates locating peg aligned with slot for removal

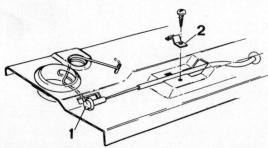

FIG 12:16   Bonnet lock release cable nipple 1 and clip 2

being 235.5mm (9.26in). Install the glass and lower it until the cable clamps can be installed and tightened through the apertures in the door inner panel. Check the tension of the cable and align the glass. Install the two lower bolts securing the glass front run channel and tighten the upper bolt. Reposition the window glass if necessary by slackening the cable clamps and adjusting accordingly. Lubricate the cable rollers with gear oil and the regulator and cable with high melting point grease. Lower the window fully to align the rear glass run channel, then tighten the bolt 10. Refit the remaining components in the reverse order of removal.

Window glass, rear doors:

On four-door saloon models the rear door window glass is controlled by a continuous cable which runs on two roller guides and is operated by a drum mechanism similar to that on the front door.

To remove the glass, refer to **FIG 12:14**, and proceed as for the front door by removing the trim pad, followed by the upper frame channel insert and rear run channel and weather strips. Unbolt the clamp and lift out the glass.

Refitting is a reverse of this process but when assembling the glass to the support channel ensure that the dimension between the single cable clamp centre line and the rear edge of the glass is 247.7mm (9.75in).

Rear door lock:

The rear door locks are locked from inside the car by a button which operates a bellcrank as shown in **FIG 12:15**. This can be removed by withdrawing two screws securing the lock mechanism and rotating the bellcrank clockwise through 90° so that the locating peg aligns with the slot.

Rear door quarter light:

Replacement of the rear quarter glass is a straight-forward operation after the window glass and channel are removed as previously described.

12:3 The bonnet

The bonnet hinges are welded to the upper dash panel and bolted to the bonnet panel. Slotted holes in the hinge arms allow for adjustment of bonnet position in the body aperture. Adjustable rubber buffers mounted on the front panel control bonnet front end height. The bonnet is secured in the closed position by a spring lock and separate safety catch, and is unlocked from inside the car by means of a cable control.

If the bonnet is difficult to close after adjusting the front end height, or if up and down movement can be felt after closing the bonnet, the dovetail spring-bolt can be adjusted. To do this, slacken the locknut at the bonnet panel and use a screwdriver in the conical end of the bolt to turn it in the required direction. When the adjustment is correct firmly tighten the locknut.

A nut and lockwasher secures the bonnet lock release outer cable to the mounting bracket inside the car. The release cable can be disconnected from the lock spring as shown in **FIG 12:16**. Release clip 2 from the upper panel and ease the cable nipple 1 out of the curled end of spring. The bonnet lock spring can be removed through the spring pivot hole after unhooking the spring anchor leg from the upper panel.

12:4 The tailgate

The tailgate is mounted on two hinges which are attached to the roof rail by two studs and nuts and welded to the tailgate inner panel. To remove the tailgate it is only necessary to remove one hinge from the roof rail and slide the other hinge from the pivot. Access to the nuts securing the hinge is gained by pulling away the weather strip and headlining. The tailgate window is of toughened glass, provided with an electric heating element printed on the interior surface. Removal of the tailgate window is carried out in the same manner as that described for the windscreen in **Section 12:5**. Before removing either the tailgate window or the tailgate assembly complete, disconnect the wires from the terminals at each side of the window glass. Take care to avoid scratching the printed circuit on the glass inner surface. If the printed circuit is accidentally damaged, repairs can be carried out with a high conductivity paint.

Two piston assemblies are provided to assist tailgate opening and to hold the tailgate in the open position. These are non-adjustable and are mounted on ball joints screwed into the tailgate inner panel and body aperture. A piston can be detached from its ball joint after removing the spring clip shown in **FIG 12:17**. When refitting, lubricate the ball joints with high melting point grease. No attempt must be made to dismantle a piston unit as the assembly contains high pressure coil springs. If a piston is faulty it must be renewed complete.

12:5 Windscreen removal

Windscreens are either of toughened or of laminated safety glass, identified by the maker's mark etched on the glass.

To remove an unbroken windscreen glass, use a broad-bladed tool to ease the inside lip of the glazing channel over the aperture flange along the top and sides of the windscreen. The glass can then be carefully pushed out complete with glazing channel and insert strip without affecting the existing glass to channel seal. Protect paintwork, ventilator grille and defrost outlets before removing damaged windscreens.

To install a windscreen, fit the glazing channel to the glass and insert strong thin cord around the securing lip groove of the channel. Leave a loop at the top of the glass, crossing the cord here and where the ends emerge at the bottom of the glass (see **FIG 12:18**). Before installing the glass, apply sealing compound all round the root of the body aperture flange. With an assistant holding the glass central in the body aperture and applying light pressure to the outside of the glass, lift the lip of the glazing channel over the aperture bottom flange by pulling the cord to within 150mm (6in) of each corner. Ensure that the glass is still central in the aperture before repeating the procedure at the top of the glass and finally at the side of the glass. After installing the glass, inject sealing compound between the outside of the glass and the glazing channel. To install the moulding in the windscreen channel a special tool No. D1163 is needed.

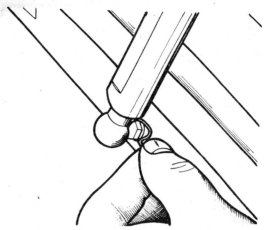

FIG 12:17 Removing spring clip from tailgate piston ball joint

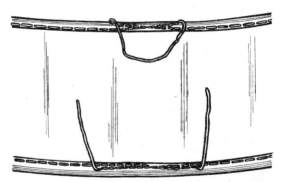

FIG 12:18 Fitting cord around glazing channel groove before windscreen installation

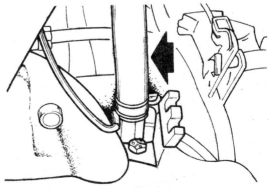

FIG 12:19 The heater hose connected to the cylinder head adaptor

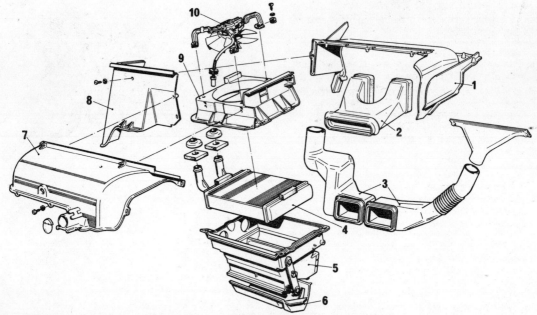

FIG 12:20 Ventilator and heater components

Key to Fig 12:20   1 Lefthand water deflector   2 Face level vent duct   3 Demist ducts   4 Heater radiator   5 Heater lower casing   6 Outlet deflector   7 Centre water deflector   8 Righthand water deflector   9 Heater upper casing   10 Heater motor and fan

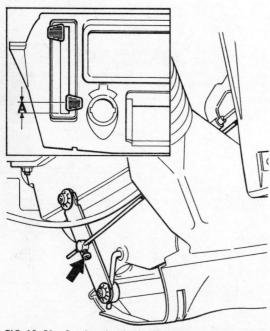

FIG 12:21 Setting the air distribution rod with control set so that dimension A is 6mm (0.24in). The adjuster screw is arrowed

Commence the installation at the top and centre of the glass. Fit the moulding sleeve over the joint. Soap solution should be applied to the channel to prevent the tool from tearing the channel lips.

12:6 Heating and ventilation system

Ventilation of the car interior with cool air is by means of face level adjustable vents in the centre of the instrument panel, supplied from an intake in the shroud panel. The air is extracted through slots provided above the tailgate. Additional ventilation is provided by an assembly mounted in the scuttle, which incorporates the heater radiator. A two-speed fan motor is attached to the ventilator assembly and serves to boost the air flow through the unit.

Bleeding the heater:

When refilling the cooling system it is occasionally possible for air to become trapped in the heater radiator, causing a substantial reduction in the flow of heated water through the radiator. If insufficient hot air is passing into the car through the heater when the engine cooling system is at normal operating temperature and the heater controls are in the maximum heat position, the heater system should be bled and the operation checked again before examining the system for faults in the heater radiator or water control valve.

With the engine switched off, completely fill the radiator with coolant and refit the filler cap. Disconnect the heater hose, arrowed in **FIG 12:19**, from the adaptor on the cylinder head and plug the adaptor to prevent loss of coolant from the engine. Move the heater control lever to the maximum heat position. Raise the end of the hose above the level of the heater and pour coolant into the hose until both heater and hose are completely filled. Add coolant slowly to allow trapped air to escape. Reconnect the heater hose to the adaptor then run the engine up to normal operating temperature and check the operation of the heater. Switch off the engine and check the level of coolant in the radiator, which should be 1in below the bottom of the radiator filler neck.

Ventilator and heater assembly:

The components of the ventilator and heater assembly are shown in **FIG 12:20**. The motor and fan 10 are mounted in the heater upper casing 9 which is secured to the scuttle panel. Righthand 8, centre 7 and lefthand 1 water deflectors, secured to the scuttle and shroud panels, deflect air through the heater casing and into the face level vent duct 2. The heater radiator 4 is mounted in the heater lower casing 5 which also houses the rod-operated air distribution flap. An outlet deflector 6 and two demist ducts 3 are clipped to the heater lower casing.

Before the heater lower casing and radiator can be withdrawn it is necessary to remove the parcel shelf and detach the outlet deflector, demist ducts, heater hoses and control cable and rod. The outlet deflector is removed by pushing the pegs out of the location holes in the lower casing and sliding the deflector towards the left of the car. The heater lower casing can be removed after detaching the four securing nuts. The heater radiator should be carefully levered out of the heater casing.

Access to the fan motor is gained after removing the centre water deflector assembly which is secured to the scuttle and shroud panel by nine screws. To detach the fan and motor, remove the two motor attaching screws that are most accessible, then loosen the third screw and withdraw the forked end of the bracket from the rubber grommet. The motor and fan are serviced only as a complete assembly, so if defective must be renewed as an assembly. When refitting, press the fan fully onto the

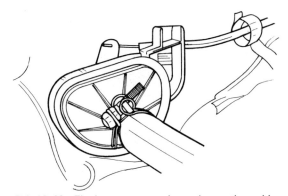

FIG 12:22 The heater water valve and operating cable

motor shaft and install the clip. Apply sealer to water deflector joint faces before installation.

When refitting the heater radiator and lower casing, apply sealer to the lower casing flange and demist duct apertures. If the lefthand water deflector is removed, ensure that sufficient sealer is applied during reassembly to provide a watertight joint between the front edge of deflector and shroud panel.

When servicing is complete, adjust the heater and ventilator controls as described next.

Adjusting controls:

Adjustment of the air distribution rod is carried out by slackening the screw arrowed in **FIG 12:21**, then setting the control lever so that dimension A is 6mm (0.24in), moving the flap operating lever fully forward, then retightening the adjuster screw.

To adjust the water valve cable, set the instrument panel heat control lever in the upward (hot) position, then move the water valve lever fully to the left of the car (see **FIG 12:22**). In this position, adjust the cable until slack is just eliminated. When installing the clip make sure that the outer cable does not restrict the water valve lever movement. Note that the water valve is a sealed assembly and must be renewed complete if defective.

NOTES

APPENDIX

Inches	Decimals	Milli-metres	Inches to Millimetres		Millimetres to Inches	
			Inches	mm	mm	Inches
1/64	.015625	.3969	.001	.0254	.01	.00039
1/32	.03125	.7937	.002	.0508	.02	.00079
3/64	.046875	1.1906	.003	.0762	.03	.00118
1/16 .0625	.0625	1.5875	.004	.1016	.04	.00157
5/64	.078125	1.9844	.005	.1270	.05	.00197
3/32	.09375	2.3812	.006	.1524	.06	.00236
7/64	.109375	2.7781	.007	.1778	.07	.00276
1/8	.125	3.1750	.008	.2032	.08	.00315
9/64	.140625	3.5719	.009	.2286	.09	.00354
5/32	.15625	3.9687	.01	.254	.1	.00394
11/64	.171875	4.3656	.02	.508	.2	.00787
3/16	.1875	4.7625	.03	.762	.3	.01181
13/64	.203125	5·1594	.04	1.016	.4	.01575
7/32	.21875	5.5562	.05	1.270	.5	.01969
15/64	.234375	5.9531	.06	1.524	.6	.02362
1/4	.25	6.3500	.07	1.778	.7	.02756
17/64	.265625	6.7469	.08	2.032	.8	.03150
9/32	.28125	7.1437	.09	2.286	.9	.03543
19/64	.296875	7.5406	.1	2.54	1	.03937
5/16	.3125	7.9375	.2	5.08	2	.07874
21/64	.328125	8.3344	.3	7.62	3	.11811
11/32	.34375	8.7312	.4	10.16	4	.15748
23/64	.359375	9.1281	.5	12.70	5	.19685
3/8	.375	9.5250	.6	15.24	6	.23622
25/64	.390625	9.9219	.7	17.78	7	.27559
13/32	.40625	10.3187	.8	20.32	8	.31496
27/64	.421875	10.7156	.9	22.86	9	.35433
7/16	.4375	11.1125	1	25.4	10	.39370
29/64	.453125	11.5094	2	50.8	11	.43307
15/32	.46875	11.9062	3	76.2	12	.47244
31/64	.484375	12.3031	4	101.6	13	.51181
1/2	.5	12.7000	5	127.0	14	.55118
33/64	.515625	13.0969	6	152.4	15	.59055
17/32	.53125	13.4937	7	177.8	16	.62992
35/64	.546875	13.8906	8	203.2	17	.66929
9/16	.5625	14.2875	9	228.6	18	.70866
37/64	.578125	14.6844	10	254.0	19	.74803
19/32	.59375	15.0812	11	279.4	20	.78740
39/64	.609375	15.4781	12	304.8	21	.82677
5/8	.625	15.8750	13	330.2	22	.86614
41/64	.640625	16.2719	14	355.6	23	.90551
21/32	.65625	16.6687	15	381.0	24	.94488
43/64	.671875	17.0656	16	406.4	25	.98425
11/16	.6875	17.4625	17	431.8	26	1.02362
45/64	.703125	17.8594	18	457.2	27	1.06299
23/32	.71875	18.2562	19	482.6	28	1.10236
47/64	.734375	18.6531	20	508.0	29	1.14173
3/4	.75	19.0500	21	533.4	30	1.18110
49/64	.765625	19.4469	22	558.8	31	1.22047
25/32	.78125	19.8437	23	584.2	32	1.25984
51/64	.796875	20.2406	24	609.6	33	1.29921
13/16	.8125	20.6375	25	635.0	34	1.33858
53/64	.828125	21.0344	26	660.4	35	1.37795
27/32	.84375	21.4312	27	685.8	36	1.41732
55/64	.859375	21.8281	28	711.2	37	1.4567
7/8	.875	22.2250	29	736.6	38	1.4961
57/64	.890625	22.6219	30	762.0	39	1.5354
29/32	.90625	23.0187	31	787.4	40	1.5748
59/64	.921875	23.4156	32	812.8	41	1.6142
15/16	.9375	23.8125	33	838.2	42	1.6535
61/64	.953125	24.2094	34	863.6	43	1.6929
31/32	.96875	24.6062	35	889.0	44	1.7323
63/64	.984375	25.0031	36	914.4	45	1.7717

UNITS	Pints to Litres	Gallons to Litres	Litres to Pints	Litres to Gallons	Miles to Kilometres	Kilometres to Miles	Lbs. per sq. In. to Kg. per sq. Cm.	Kg. per sq. Cm. to Lbs. per sq. In.
1	.57	4.55	1.76	.22	1.61	.62	.07	14.22
2	1.14	9.09	3.52	.44	3.22	1.24	.14	28.50
3	1.70	13.64	5.28	.66	4.83	1.86	.21	42.67
4	2.27	18.18	7.04	.88	6.44	2.49	.28	56.89
5	2.84	22.73	8.80	1.10	8.05	3.11	.35	71.12
6	3.41	27.28	10.56	1.32	9.66	3.73	.42	85.34
7	3.98	31.82	12.32	1.54	11.27	4.35	.49	99.56
8	4.55	36.37	14.08	1.76	12.88	4.97	.56	113.79
9		40.91	15.84	1.98	14.48	5.59	.63	128.00
10		45.46	17.60	2.20	16.09	6.21	.70	142.23
20				4.40	32.19	12.43	1.41	284.47
30				6.60	48.28	18.64	2.11	426.70
40				8.80	64.37	24.85		
50					80.47	31.07		
60					96.56	37.28		
70					112.65	43.50		
80					128.75	49.71		
90					144.84	55.92		
100					160.93	62.14		

UNITS	Lb ft to kgm	Kgm to lb ft	UNITS	Lb ft to kgm	Kgm to lb ft
1	.138	7.233	7	.967	50.631
2	.276	14.466	8	1.106	57.864
3	.414	21.699	9	1.244	65.097
4	.553	28.932	10	1.382	72.330
5	.691	36.165	20	2.765	144.660
6	.829	43.398	30	4.147	216.990

TECHNICAL DATA

ENGINE

Capacity	1256cc (76.6cu in)
Firing order	1-3-4-2
Compression ratio:	
Standard compression	9.2:1. On later models 8.7:1
Low compression	7.3:1
Cylinder head:	
Permissible distortion on attachment face:	
Longitudinally	0.13mm (0.005in) maximum
Transversely	0.08mm (0.003in) maximum
Manifold attachment faces	0.05mm (0.002in) maximum
Permissible depth of cylinder head after refacing:	
Standard compression engine	81.10 mm (3.193in) minimum
Low compression engine	81.81mm (3.221in) minimum
Valve seating angle	45°
Valve seating width:	
Intake	1.3 to 1.5mm (0.05 to 0.06in)
Exhaust	1.5 to 2.0mm (0.06 to 0.08in)
Valves:	
Stem diameter, standards:	
Intake	6.980 to 6.998mm (0.2748 to 0.2755in)
Exhaust	6.972 to 6.990mm (0.2745 to 0.2752in)
Stem clearance in guide:	
Intake	0.013 to 0.051mm (0.0005 to 0.0020in)
Exhaust	0.033 to 0.071mm (0.0013 to 0.0028in)
Seat angle	44°
Valve head thickness:	
Intake	0.8mm (0.03in) minimum
Exhaust	1.0mm (0.04in) minimum
Valve springs:	
Assembled height	34mm (1.34in) maximum
Free length, nominal	38mm (1.5in)
Spring load at 33.5mm (1.32in)	196 to 231N (44 to 52lbf)
Valve tappets:	
Diameter	11.968 to 11.984mm (0.4712 to 0.4718in)
Clearance in guide	0.015 to 0.048mm (0.0006 to 0.0019in)
Valve clearance, hot:	
Intake and exhaust	0.2mm (0.008in)
Valve timing:	
Intake valve maximum opening point	107° after TDC
Camshaft and bearings:	
Journal diameter:	
Front	40.963 to 40.975mm (1.6127 to 1.6132in)
Centre	40.462 to 40.475mm (1.5930 to 1.5935in)
Rear	39.962 to 39.975mm (1.5733 to 1.5738in)

Clearance in bearings	0.025 to 0.064mm (0.0010 to 0.0025in)
End float	0.05 to 0.23mm (0.002 to 0.009in)
Thrust plate thickness	3.12 to 3.20mm (0.123 to 0.126in)
Permissible dimension, cam peak to base ..	33.07mm (1.302in) minimum

Cylinder block:

Cylinder bore diameter, nominal standard ..	80.98mm (3.188in)
Permissible depth of block after refacing (top face to main bearing cap face)	190.7mm (7.508in) minimum
Permissible distortion on top face:	
Longitudinally	0.13mm (0.005in) maximum
Transversely	0.08mm (0.003in) maximum

Piston rings:

Ring gap in cylinder bore	0.23 to 0.51mm (0.009 to 0.020in)
Thickness (top to bottom face):	
Top and centre rings	1.96 to 1.98mm (0.077 to 0.078in)
Clearance in piston groove:	
Top ring	0.048 to 0.099mm (0.0019 to 0.0039in)
Centre ring	0.041 to 0.091mm (0.0016 to 0.0036in)

Piston pins:

Clearance in piston bosses at 20°C	0.006 to 0.011mm (0.00025 to 0.00045in)

Pistons:

Clearance in cylinder bore	0.023 to 0.036mm (0.0009 to 0.0014in)

Connecting rods:

Bearing housing bore	48.158 to 48.171mm (1.8960 to 1.8965in)
End float on crankpin	0.10 to 0.25mm (0.004 to 0.010in)

Crankshaft and bearings:

Crankpin diameter, standard	46.487 to 46.505mm (1.8302 to 1.8310in)
Crankpin clearance in bearing	0.025 to 0.074mm (0.0010 to 0.0029in)
Crankpin fillet radius	2.29 to 2.67mm (0.090 to 0.105in)
Crank throw	30.40 to 30.53mm (1.197 to 1.202in)
Main journal diameter, standard	53.988 to 54.000mm (2.1255 to 2.1260in)
Main journal clearance in bearing	0.025 to 0.064mm (0.001 to 0.0025in)
Main journal fillet radius	2.29 to 2.67mm (0.090 to 0.105in)
Crankshaft end float	0.05 to 0.20mm (0.002 to 0.008in)
Permissible crankshaft run-out	0.038mm (0.0015in) maximum
Main bearing housing bores	58.001 to 58.014mm (2.2835 to 2.2840in)
Centre main bearing width	32.69 to 32.74mm (1.287 to 1.289in)

Oil pump:

Driving impeller spindle:	
Diameter	10.991 to 11.034mm (0.4327 to 0.4344in)
End float	0.18 to 0.25mm (0.007 to 0.010in)
Clearance in pump body	0.015 to 0.043mm (0.0006 to 0.0017in)
Driven impeller spindle diameter	10.930 to 10.940mm (0.4303 to 0.4307in)

Impellers:
End clearance in body	0.05 to 0.13mm (0.002 to 0.005in)
Radial clearance in body	0.05 to 0.13mm (0.002 to 0.005in)
Backlash between teeth	0.10 to 0.20mm (0.004 to 0.008in)
Clearance on driven spindle	0.008 to 0.038mm (0.0003 to 0.0015in)

Oil pressure relief valve:
Plunger diameter	11.057 to 11.069mm (0.4353 to 0.4358in)
Plunger clearance in cover	0.030 to 0.069mm (0.0012 to 0.0027in)
Spring free length	49.8mm (1.96in)
Spring load at 27.1mm (1.66in)	35.0 to 37.5N (7lb 15ozf to 8lb 4ozf)

CLUTCH

Fork free travel 6mm (0.24in)

Pedal shaft:
Shaft diameter	13.96 to 14.00mm (0.550 to 0.551in)
Clearance in bush	0.12 to 0.23mm (0.005 to 0.009in)

Disc hub springs:
Number	4
Identification colour	Cream

FUEL SYSTEM

Fuel grade:
Standard compression engine	97 octane minimum
Low compression engine	90 octane minimum

Fuel pump pressure .. .. 0.17 to 0.24 bar (2½ to 3½lbf/sq in)

Carburetter:

Identification:
Standard compression engine	3696B. 3946B from engine no 1817784
Low compression engine	3698
Metering needle	B1DV. BIEU from engine no 1817784
Jet orifice	2.54mm
Air valve spring identification colour	Natural
Fast-idle cam	M2
Needle valve	1.5mm
Needle valve washer thickness	1.6mm
Float position	See text
Engine idling speed	800 to 850rev/min

COOLING SYSTEM

Fan belt tension (used belt) .. .. .. 330N (75lbf) tension gauge reading or 7mm (0.28) deflection under thumb pressure applied midway between alternator and water pump
For a new belt the figures are 400N (90lbf) and 5mm (0.20in) deflection

Thermostat:

Valve opening temperature .. .. .. 88°C. 92°C on some later models

Radiator:
Leak test pressure	1.4 bar (20lbf/sq in)
Filler cap pressure valve opening pressure	0.94 to 1.21 bar (13½ to 17½ lbf/sq in)

IGNITION SYSTEM

Distributor:

Circuit breaker contact gap setting:

New contacts	0.55mm (0.022in)
Used contacts	0.50mm (0.020in)
Contact arm spring tension	5.3 to 6.7N (19 to 24ozf)
Cam dwell angle	49° to 51°

Circuit breaker plate:

Force required to rotate upper plate	2.8 to 4.4N (10 to 16ozf)

Mainshaft:

Diameter	12.43 to 12.45mm (0.4895 to 0.4900in)
Clearance in bushes	0.008 to 0.033mm (0.0003 to 0.0013in)
End float	0.05 to 0.13mm (0.002 to 0.005in)
Ignition timing	9° BTDC

Spark plugs:

Type	AC 42XLS, 41 4XLS on later models
Plug gap	1.0mm (0.040in)

TRANSMISSION

Mainshaft second and third speed gears:

Mainshaft diameter	27.915 to 27.927mm (1.0990 to 1.0095in)
Gear clearance on shaft	0.036 to 0.071mm (0.0014 to 0.0028in)

Countershaft gear:

Overall length	152.91 to 152.96mm (6.020 to 6.022in)
Thrust washer thickness	1.562 to 1.613mm (0.0615 to 0.0635in)
End float in casing	0.15 to 0.36mm (0.006 to 0.014in)

Reverse pinion:

Pinion shaft diameter	14.023 to 14.041mm (0.5521 to 0.5528in)
Pinion clearance on shaft	0.056 to 0.099mm (0.0022 to 0.0039in)

PROPELLER SHAFT

Sliding sleeve:

Sleeve diameter	28.549 to 28.575mm (1.124 to 1.125in)
Sleeve clearance in transmission rear cover bush	0.038 to 0.102mm (0.0015 to 0.0040in)

REAR AXLE

Pinion bearings:

Pre-load:

New bearings	0.50 to 1.20Nm (4.4 to 10.8lbf in)
Used bearings	0.30 to 0.60Nm (2.6 to 5.3lbf in)

Differential and hypoid gear:

Pinion shaft diameter	15.973 to 16.000mm (0.6289 to 0.6299in)
Pinion clearance on shaft	0.043 to 0.150mm (0.0017 to 0.0059in)

Side bearing pre-load:	
New bearings	17.8N (4lbf)
Used bearings .. '..	5.6N (1.25lbf)
Permissible run-out of differential case flange ..	0.025mm (0.001in)
Permissible run-out of hypoid gear	0.08mm (0.003in)
Hypoid gear and pinion backlash	0.10 to 0.20mm (0.004 to 0.008in)

FRONT AXLE, STEERING AND ROAD WHEELS

*Steering geometry:

Front wheel alignment	12' to 32' toe-in, equivalent to 1.0 to 3.0mm (0.04 to 0.12in) at wheel rims
Camber angle	* **0° 15' positive to 1° 15' negative
Steering pivot inclination	*8°
Caster angle	* **5° positive to 2° 30' positive
Toe-out on turns	Outside wheel 18° 15' to 19° 45' from straightahead with inside wheel at 20°

*With car standing level within 6.1mm (0.24in) side for side at the front and rear
**To be within 1° side for side

Front hubs:

Bearing end float	0.02 to 0.10mm (0.001 to 0.004in)

Wheels:

Permissible lateral run-out, checked on vertical inside face of flange	1mm (0.04in) maximum
Permissible radial run-out, checked on tyre seat face of flange	1mm (0.04in) maximum

Tyre pressures:

155 SR 13	21 lb/sq in (front), 25lb/sq in (rear)

BRAKES

Pedal shaft and bush:

Shaft diameter	13.96 to 14.00mm (0.550 to 0.551in)
Clearance in bush	0.12 to 0.23mm (0.005 to 0.009in)

Brake drums:

Permissible diameter after service refacing ..	201mm (7.913in)
Permissible run-out of drum braking surface, checked on axle shaft	0.08mm (0.003in)

Disc brake pads:

Permissible thickness of friction material ..	1.5mm (0.06in) minimum

Brake discs:

Permissible run-out	0.1mm (0.004in)
Permissible thickness after service refacing	9.9mm (0.39in)

ELECTRICAL SYSTEM

Battery:

Standard, 40 amp hour at 20 hour	Exide 6-VTAZ9BR or Lucas 3A9
Large capacity, 55 amp hour at 20 hour rate ..	Exide 6XW11L

Delco-Remy DN 460 alternator:

Voltage	12
Output	35 amp
Field resistance (± 5%)	2.8ohms
Brush minimum length	5mm (0.2in)
Brush spring pressure	2.2 to 3.6N (8 to 13ozf)

Slip rings:

Maximum eccentricity	0.05mm (0.002in)
Minimum diameter	21.95mm (0.864in)

Lucas M35J/I starter:
Brush length .. .. 9.5mm (0.38in) minimum
Commutator permissible thickness after skimming 2mm (0.08in) minimum
Starter test data:
    Free running current .. .. 50 amp at 8000 to 10,000rev/min at 12 volts
    Lock torque .. .. 9Nm (6.7lbf ft) at 365 amp

Lucas 5M90/PE starter:
Brush length .. .. 9.5mm (0.38in) minimum
Commutator permissible thickness after skimming 2mm (0.08in) minimum
Armature shaft end float .. .. 0.25mm (0.010in) maximum
Solenoid switch test data:
    Series winding resistance .. .. .. 0.21 to 0.25ohms
    Shunt winding resistance .. .. .. 0.9 to 1.1ohms
Starter test data:
    Free running current .. .. 65 amp at 8000 to 11,500 rev/min at 12 volts
    Lock torque .. .. • .. 10.8Nm (8lbf ft) at 370 amp

Wiper motor:
Total light running current consumption, warm:
    High speed .. .. 5 amp
    Low speed .. .. 2.5 amp
Wiper arm spring tension.. .. .. .. 5.3N (19ozf)

Lamp bulbs:
	Watts
Headlamps	45/40
Sidelamps	4
Tail/stop	5/21
Indicator lamps	21
Side repeater lamps	4
Licence plate	5
Reversing light	21
Fog lamps	55 quartz halogen H3
Interior light	10 festoon type
Instrument warning light	1.2
Alternator warning lamp	3

CAPACITIES

Engine oil pan:
Dry engine .. .. 3.1 litres (5.5 UK pints)
Refill with filter element change .. .. .. 2.8 litres (5 UK pints)
Refill .. .. 2.5 litres (4.5 UK pints)
Cooling system:
With heater .. .. 5.7 litres (10 UK pints)
Transmission .. .. 0.51 litre (0.9 UK pint)
Rear axle .. .. 0.60 litre (1.0 UK pints)

LUBRICATION

Engine oil:
    Multigrade oil to GM spec. 6136M
    Ambient temperatures:
      Above 0°C .. .. SAE 10W/40, 10W/50, 20W/40, 20W/50
      0°C to −12°C .. .. .. SAE 10W/30, 10W/40, 10W/50
      Below −12°C .. .. SAE 5W/30
Gearbox, GM spec. 4753M .. .. .. SAE 80
Rear axle, GM spec. 4655M .. .. .. Hypoid SAE 90

TORQUE WRENCH SETTINGS

Engine and clutch:
- Connecting rod bolts .. .. *34Nm (25lbf ft)
- Crankshaft main bearing bolts .. .. .. *111Nm (82lbf ft)
- Flywheel bolts .. ..**41Nm (30lbf ft)
- Cylinder head bolts .. .. 74Nm (55lbf ft)
- Oil filter bolt .. .. 19Nm (14lbf ft)
- Engine front mountings and nuts .. .. 39Nm (29lbf ft)
- Engine rear mounting:
  - Mounting to transmission bolt.. .. .. 45Nm (32lbf ft)
  - Crossmember to body bracket bolts .. .. 40Nm (28lbf ft)
- Clutch to flywheel bolts .. .. .. 20Nm (14lbf ft)
- Spark plugs .. .. 34Nm (25lbf ft)

* Oiled threads   ** Sealed threads

Rear axle and rear suspension:
- Axle shaft bearing retainer plate nuts .. .. *26Nm (19lbf ft)
- Wheel nuts .. .. *65Nm (48lbf ft)
- Pinion extension housing to axle housing bolts .. 27Nm (20lbf ft)
- Pinion extension shaft flange nut .. .. 25Nm (18lbf ft)
- Panhard rod to body mounting bolt .. .. 98Nm (72lbf ft)
- Panhard rod to axle nut .. .. 64Nm (47lbf ft)
- Suspension arm bolts .. .. 67Nm (50lbf ft)
- Pinion extension housing to crossmember bolts .. 20Nm (15lbf ft)
- Shock absorber lower mounting nuts .. .. 43Nm (32lbf ft)

* Clean dry threads

Front axle and front suspension:
- Upper arm fulcrum bolts .. .. 80Nm (59lbf ft)
- Lower arm fulcrum bolts .. .. 66Nm (49lbf ft)
- Lower arm outrigger fulcrum bolts .. .. 66Nm (49lbf ft)
- Axle inner mounting bolts .. .. .. 64Nm (47lbf ft)
- Axle outer mounting bolts .. .. .. 74Nm (55lbf ft)
- Upper ball joint retaining nuts .. .. .. 40Nm (30lbf ft)
- Stabiliser bar mounting bolts .. .. .. 20Nm (15lbf ft)
- Shock absorber lower mounting bolts .. .. 40Nm (30lbf ft)

Steering:
- Steering wheel nut .. .. 60Nm (44lbf ft)
- Column upper support bracket nuts .. .. 14Nm (10lbf ft)
- Column lower mount bolt .. .. .. See text
- Steering coupling pinch bolt .. .. .. 17Nm (13lbf ft)
- Pinion shaft retaining nut .. .. .. 15Nm (11lbf ft)
- Rack pre-load adjusting screw locknut .. .. 68Nm (50lbf ft)
- Tie rod inner ball joint to rack .. .. .. 90Nm (66lbf ft)
- Steering gear mounting bolts .. .. .. 20Nm (15lbf ft)

Brakes:
- Brake caliper to steering knuckle bolts .. 98Nm (72lbf ft)
- Brake disc to hub bolts .. .. 40Nm (30lbf ft)
- Master cylinder secondary port connector .. 37Nm (27lbf ft)
- Rear brake flange plate nuts .. .. .. 26Nm (19lbf ft)
- Rear brake adjuster pre-load .. .. .. 3.1 to 3.9Nm (27 to 35lbf in)

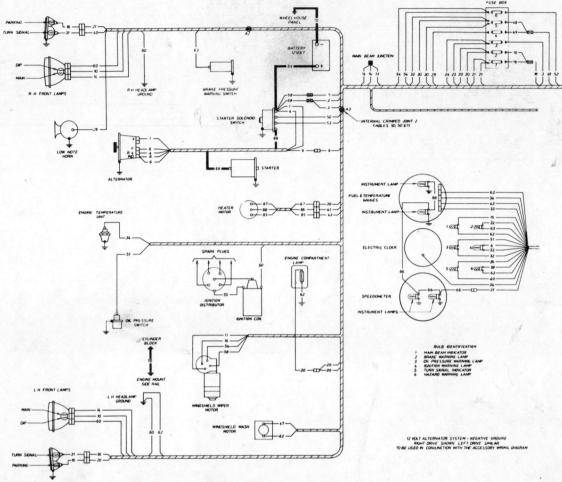

FIG 13:1   Physical wiring diagram

Key to colour code and wire sizes:

No.	Colour	Size	No.	Colour	Size	No.	Colour	Size
1	Brown	65/0.30	25	Purple/brown	14/0.30	49	White	28/0.30
2	Brown	44/0.30	26	Purple/white	9/0.30	50	White	14/0.30
3	Brown	35/0.30	27	Purple/black	14/0.30	51	White/brown	9/0.30
4	Brown	14/0.30	28	Purple/black	9/0.30	52	White/blue	28/0.30
5	Brown/blue	35/0.30	29	Green	28/0.30	53	White/red	28/0.30
6	Brown/yellow	9/0.30	30	Green	14/0.30	54	White/green	14/0.30
7	Blue	35/0.30	31	Green	14/0.25	55	White/black	7/16/0.10
8	Blue	28/0.30	32	Green	9/0.30	56	White/black	28/0.30
9	Blue/red	28/0.30	33	Green/brown	9/0.30	57	White/black	9/0.30
10	Blue/red	14/0.30	34	Green/blue	9/0.30	58	Yellow/light green	14/0.30
11	Blue/light green	14/0.30	35	Green/red	14/0.30	59	Black	28/0.30
12	Blue/white	35/0.30	36	Green/red	9/0.30	60	Black	14/0.30
13	Blue/white	28/0.30	37	Green/purple	9/0.30	61	Black	14/0.25
14	Blue/white	14/0.30	38	Green/light green	9/0.30	62	Black	9/0.30
15	Blue/white	9/0.30	39	Green/white	14/0.30	63	Black/white	9/0.30
16	Red	14/0.25	40	Green/white	9/0.30	64	Brown/white	0.75mm²
17	Red/blue	9/0.30	41	Green/yellow	14/0.30	65	Yellow	0.75mm²
18	Red/green	28/0.30	42	Green/black	9/0.30	66	Grey	0.75mm²
19	Red/light green	14/0.30	43	Green/slate	14/0.30	67	Black	0.75mm²
20	Red/black	9/0.30	44	Light green/brown	14/0.30	68	Fusible link	14/0.30
21	Red/orange	9/0.30	45	Light green/brown	9/0.30	69	Battery cable	37/0.75
22	Purple	35/0.30	46	Light green/black	14/0.25	70	Ground cable	16/16/0.30
23	Purple	28/0.30	47	Light green/black	9/0.30	71	Resistance wire	
24	Purple	9/0.30	48	White	35/0.30			

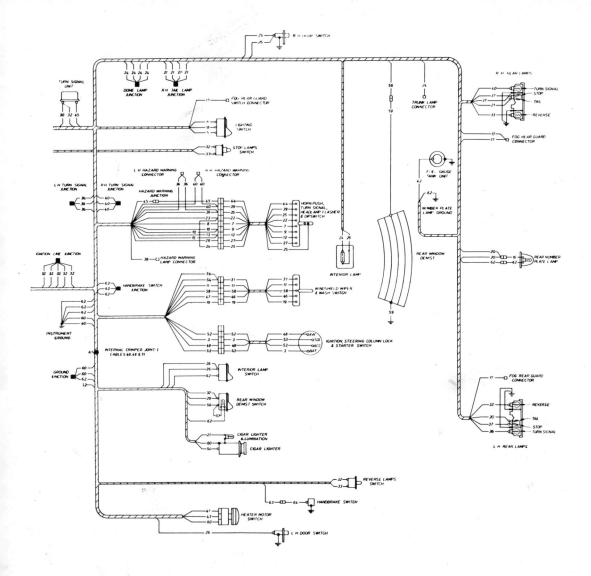

● Denotes single strand resistance wire giving a total of 2Ω ± 20Ω routed between points A1-A2-A3
Resistance wire 1/0, 71 or 22 SWG
Resistance per 25mm 0.0312Ω ± 5 per cent

Symbols

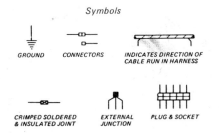

GROUND	CONNECTORS	INDICATES DIRECTION OF CABLE RUN IN HARNESS

CRIMPED SOLDERED & INSULATED JOINT	EXTERNAL JUNCTION	PLUG & SOCKET

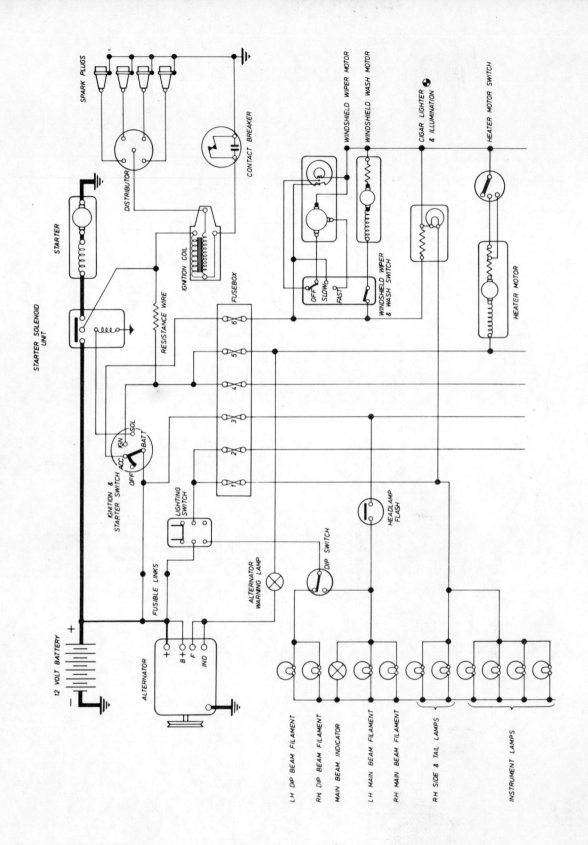

SPARK PLUGS

DISTRIBUTOR

CONTACT BREAKER

IGNITION COIL

STARTER

STARTER SOLENOID UNIT

RESISTANCE WIRE

WINDSHIELD WIPER MOTOR

WINDSHIELD WASH MOTOR

CIGAR LIGHTER & ILLUMINATION

HEATER MOTOR SWITCH

FUSEBOX

OFF
SLOW
FAST

WINDSHIELD WIPER & WASH SWITCH

HEATER MOTOR

6
5
4
3
2
1

SOL
IGN
ACC
BATT
OFF

IGNITION & STARTER SWITCH

LIGHTING SWITCH

ALTERNATOR WARNING LAMP

DIP SWITCH

HEADLAMP FLASH

FUSIBLE LINKS

12 VOLT BATTERY

+
B+
F
IND

ALTERNATOR

LH DIP BEAM FILAMENT

RH DIP BEAM FILAMENT

MAIN BEAM INDICATOR

LH MAIN BEAM FILAMENT

RH MAIN BEAM FILAMENT

RH SIDE & TAIL LAMPS

INSTRUMENT LAMPS

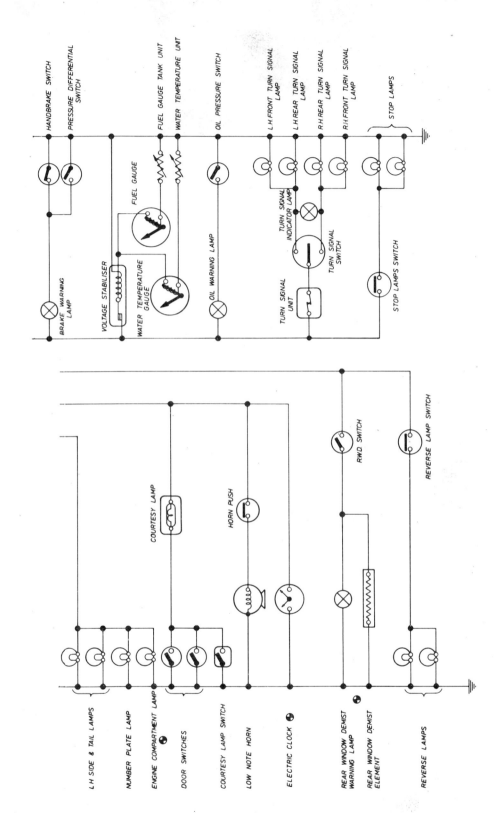

FIG 13:2 Theoretical wiring diagram

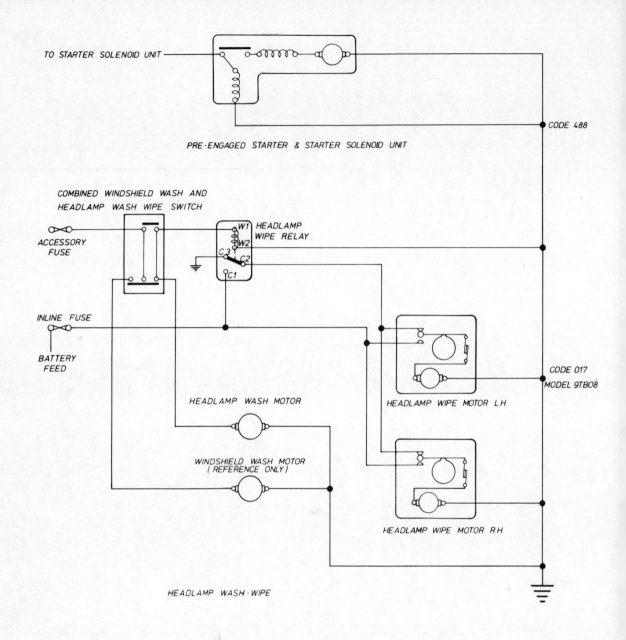

TO STARTER SOLENOID UNIT

CODE 488

PRE-ENGAGED STARTER & STARTER SOLENOID UNIT

COMBINED WINDSHIELD WASH AND
HEADLAMP WASH WIPE SWITCH

ACCESSORY
FUSE

W1
W2
HEADLAMP
WIPE RELAY

C3
C2
C1

INLINE FUSE

BATTERY
FEED

CODE 017
MODEL 9TB08

HEADLAMP WASH MOTOR

HEADLAMP WIPE MOTOR L.H.

WINDSHIELD WASH MOTOR
(REFERENCE ONLY)

HEADLAMP WIPE MOTOR R.H.

HEADLAMP WASH-WIPE

FIG 13:3 Optional equipment, theoretical wiring diagram

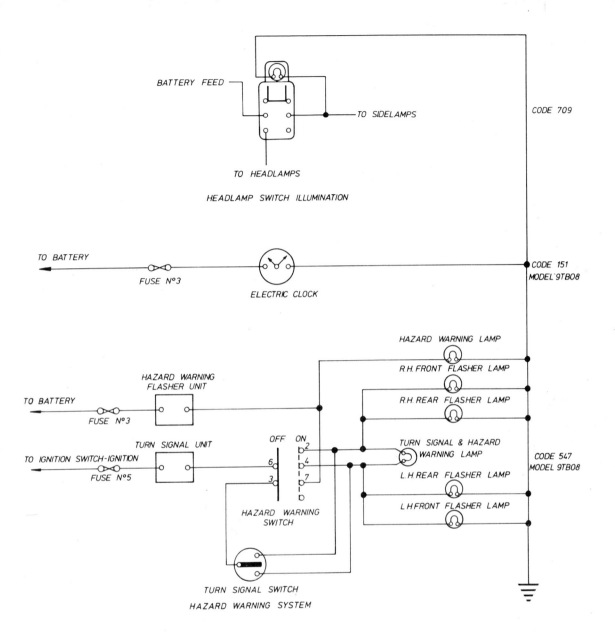

BATTERY FEED

TO SIDELAMPS

CODE 709

TO HEADLAMPS

HEADLAMP SWITCH ILLUMINATION

TO BATTERY

FUSE N°3

ELECTRIC CLOCK

CODE 151
MODEL 9TB08

HAZARD WARNING LAMP

R.H. FRONT FLASHER LAMP

HAZARD WARNING
FLASHER UNIT

TO BATTERY

FUSE N°3

R.H. REAR FLASHER LAMP

TURN SIGNAL UNIT

OFF   ON

TO IGNITION SWITCH-IGNITION

FUSE N°5

6

3

2

4

7

TURN SIGNAL & HAZARD
WARNING LAMP

L.H. REAR FLASHER LAMP

L.H. FRONT FLASHER LAMP

CODE 547
MODEL 9TB08

HAZARD WARNING
SWITCH

TURN SIGNAL SWITCH

HAZARD WARNING SYSTEM

FIG 13:3   Optional equipment, theoretical wiring diagram

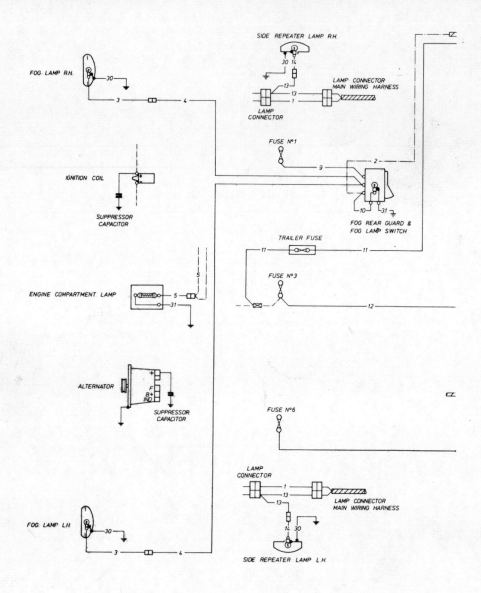

FIG 13:4   Optional equipment and accessory physical wiring diagram

Key to colour code and wire sizes:

No.	Colour	Size	No.	Colour	Size	No.	Colour	Size
1	Red	9/0.30	13	Green	9/0.30	25	Light green/brown	14/0.25
2	Red/blue	9/0.30	14	Green	14/0.25	26	Light green/brown	9/0.30
3	Red/yellow	14/0.25	15	Green/red	14/0.25	27	Light green/purple	14/0.25
4	Red/yellow	14/0.30	16	Green/red	9/0.30	28	White/green	9/0.30
5	Red/black	9/0.30	17	Green/red	14/0.30	29	White/green	14/0.30
6	Red/black	14/0.30	18	Green/purple	9/0.30	30	Black	14/0.25
7	Red/orange	9/0.30	19	Green/purple	14/0.30	31	Black	9/0.30
8	Red/orange	14/0.30	20	Green/light green	14/0.25	32	Black	14/0.30
9	Red/orange	28/0.30	21	Green/light green	9/0.30	33	Green	14/0.30
10	Red/green	9/0.30	22	Green/white	9/0.30	34	Green/brown	14/0.30
11	Purple	28/0.30	23	Green/white	14/0.25	35	Light green/orange	9/0.30
12	Purple	14/0.30	24	Green/white	14/0.30			

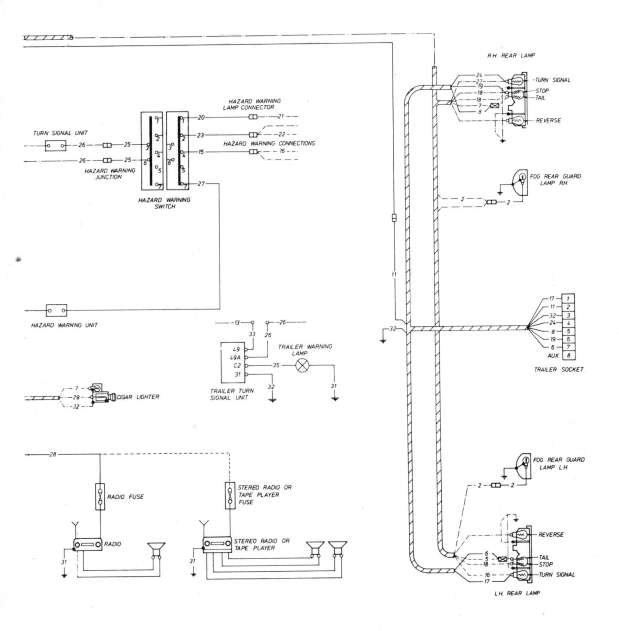

RH REAR LAMP

24 — TURN SIGNAL
22
19 — STOP
18 — TAIL
7
8

REVERSE

HAZARD WARNING
LAMP CONNECTOR

20 — 21

23 — 22

HAZARD WARNING CONNECTIONS

15 — 16

TURN SIGNAL UNIT

26 — 25

26 — 25

HAZARD WARNING
JUNCTION

HAZARD WARNING
SWITCH

27

FOG REAR GUARD
LAMP RH

2 — 2

11

HAZARD WARNING UNIT

13 — 26

33   26

TRAILER WARNING
LAMP

49
49A
C2
31

35

TRAILER TURN
SIGNAL UNIT

32   31

7

29   CIGAR LIGHTER

32

17 — 1
11 — 2
32 — 3
24 — 4
8 — 5
19 — 6
6 — 7

AUX 8

TRAILER SOCKET

32

28

RADIO FUSE

STEREO RADIO OR
TAPE PLAYER
FUSE

RADIO

31

STEREO RADIO OR
TAPE PLAYER

31

FOG REAR GUARD
LAMP LH.

2 — 2

REVERSE

6 — TAIL
5
18 — STOP
16 — TURN SIGNAL
17

LH. REAR LAMP

To be used in conjunction with main and theoretical wiring diagrams

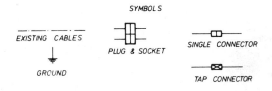

SYMBOLS

EXISTING CABLES

GROUND

PLUG & SOCKET

SINGLE CONNECTOR

TAP CONNECTOR

CHEVETTE

NOTES

HINTS ON MAINTENANCE AND OVERHAUL

There are few things more rewarding than the restoration of a vehicle's original peak of efficiency and smooth performance.

The following notes are intended to help the owner to reach that state of perfection. Providing that he possesses the basic manual skills he should have no difficulty in performing most of the operations detailed in this manual. It must be stressed, however, that where recommended in the manual, highly-skilled operations ought to be entrusted to experts, who have the necessary equipment, to carry out the work satisfactorily.

Quality of workmanship:

The hazardous driving conditions on the roads to-day demand that vehicles should be as nearly perfect, mechanically, as possible. It is therefore most important that amateur work be carried out with care, bearing in mind the often inadequate working conditions, and also the inferior tools which may have to be used. It is easy to counsel perfection in all things, and we recognize that it may be setting an impossibly high standard. We do, however, suggest that every care should be taken to ensure that a vehicle is as safe to take on the road as it is humanly possible to make it.

Safe working conditions:

Even though a vehicle may be stationary, it is still potentially dangerous if certain sensible precautions are not taken when working on it while it is supported on jacks or blocks. It is indeed preferable not to use jacks alone, but to supplement them with carefully placed blocks, so that there will be plenty of support if the car rolls off the jacks during a strenuous manoeuvre. Axle stands are an excellent way of providing a rigid base which is not readily disturbed. Piles of bricks are a dangerous substitute. Be careful not to get under heavy loads on lifting tackle, the load could fall. It is preferable not to work alone when lifting an engine, or when working underneath a vehicle which is supported well off the ground. To be trapped, particularly under the vehicle, may have unpleasant results if help is not quickly forthcoming. Make some provision, however humble, to deal with fires. Always disconnect a battery if there is a likelihood of electrical shorts. These may start a fire if there is leaking fuel about. This applies particularly to leads which can carry a heavy current, like those in the starter circuit. While on the subject of electricity, we must also stress the danger of using equipment which is run off the mains and which has no earth or has faulty wiring or connections. So many workshops have damp floors, and electrical shocks are of such a nature that it is sometimes impossible to let go of a live lead or piece of equipment due to the muscular spasms which take place.

Work demanding special care:

This involves the servicing of braking, steering and suspension systems. On the road, failure of the braking system may be disastrous. Make quite sure that there can be no possibility of failure through the bursting of rusty brake pipes or rotten hoses, nor to a sudden loss of pressure due to defective seals or valves.

Problems:

The chief problems which may face an operator are:
1 External dirt.
2 Difficulty in undoing tight fixings
3 Dismantling unfamiliar mechanisms.
4 Deciding in what respect parts are defective.
5 Confusion about the correct order for reassembly.
6 Adjusting running clearances.
7 Road testing.
8 Final tuning.

Practical suggestions to solve the problems:

1 Preliminary cleaning of large parts—engines, transmissions, steering, suspensions, etc.,—should be carried out before removal from the car. Where road dirt and mud alone are present, wash clean with a high-pressure water jet, brushing to remove stubborn adhesions, and allow to drain and dry. Where oil or grease is also present, wash down with a proprietary compound (Gunk, Teepol etc.,) applying with a stiff brush—an old paint brush is suitable—into all crevices. Cover the distributor and ignition coils with a polythene bag and then apply a strong water jet to clear the loosened deposits. Allow to drain and dry. The assemblies will then be sufficiently clean to remove and transfer to the bench for the next stage.

On the bench, further cleaning can be carried out, first wiping the parts as free as possible from grease with old newspaper. Avoid using rag or cotton waste which can leave clogging fibres behind. Any remaining grease can be removed with a brush dipped in paraffin. If necessary, traces of paraffin can be removed by carbon tetrachloride. Avoid using paraffin or petrol in large quantities for cleaning in enclosed areas, such as garages, on account of the high fire risk.

When all exteriors have been cleaned, and not before, dismantling can be commenced. This ensures that dirt will not enter into interiors and orifices revealed by dismantling. In the next phases, where components have to be cleaned, use carbon tetrachloride in preference to petrol and keep the containers covered except when in use. After the components have been cleaned, plug small holes with tapered hard wood plugs cut to size and blank off larger orifices with grease-proof paper and masking tape. Do not use soft wood plugs or matchsticks as they may break.

2 It is not advisable to hammer on the end of a screw thread, but if it must be done, first screw on a nut to protect the thread, and use a lead hammer. This applies particularly to the removal of tapered cotters. Nuts and bolts seem to 'grow' together, especially in exhaust systems. If penetrating oil does not work, try the judicious application of heat, but be careful of starting a fire. Asbestos sheet or cloth is useful to isolate heat.

Tight bushes or pieces of tail-pipe rusted into a silencer can be removed by splitting them with an open-ended hacksaw. Tight screws can sometimes be started by a tap from a hammer on the end of a suitable screwdriver. Many tight fittings will yield to the judicious use of a hammer, but it must be a soft-faced hammer if damage is to be avoided, use a heavy block on the opposite side to absorb shock. Any parts of the steering system which have been damaged should be renewed, as attempts to repair them may lead to cracking and subsequent failure, and steering ball joints should be disconnected using a recommended tool to prevent damage.

3 If often happens that an owner is baffled when trying to dismantle an unfamiliar piece of equipment. So many modern devices are pressed together or assembled by spinning-over flanges, that they must be sawn apart. The intention is that the whole assembly must be renewed. However, parts which appear to be in one piece to the naked eye, may reveal close-fitting joint lines when inspected with a magnifying glass, and, this may provide the necessary clue to dismantling. Left-handed screw threads are used where rotational forces would tend to unscrew a righthanded screw thread.

Be very careful when dismantling mechanisms which may come apart suddenly. Work in an enclosed space where the parts will be contained, and drape a piece of cloth over the device if springs are likely to fly in all directions. Mark everything which might be reassembled in the wrong position, scratched symbols may be used on unstressed parts, or a sequence of tiny dots from a centre punch can be useful. Stressed parts should never be scratched or centre-popped as this may lead to cracking under working conditions. Store parts which look alike in the correct order for reassembly. Never rely upon memory to assist in the assembly of complicated mechanisms, especially when they will be dismantled for a long time, but make notes, and drawings to supplement the diagrams in the manual, and put labels on detached wires. Rust stains may indicate unlubricated wear. This can sometimes be seen round the outside edge of a bearing cup in a universal joint. Look for bright rubbing marks on parts which normally should not make heavy contact. These might prove that something is bent or running out of truth. For example, there might be bright marks on one side of a piston, at the top near the ring grooves, and others at the bottom of the skirt on the other side. This could well be the clue to a bent connecting rod. Suspected cracks can be proved by heating the component in a light oil to approximately 100°C, removing, drying off, and dusting with french chalk, if a crack is present the oil retained in the crack will stain the french chalk.

4 In determining wear, and the degree, against the permissible limits set in the manual, accurate measurement can only be achieved by the use of a micrometer. In many cases, the wear is given to the fourth place of decimals; that is in ten-thousandths of an inch. This can be read by the vernier scale on the barrel of a good micrometer. Bore diameters are more difficult to determine. If, however, the matching shaft is accurately measured, the degree of play in the bore can be felt as a guide to its suitability. In other cases, the shank of a twist drill of known diameter is a handy check.

Many methods have been devised for determining the clearance between bearing surfaces. To-day the best and simplest is by the use of Plastigage, obtainable from most garages. A thin plastic thread is laid between the two surfaces and the bearing is tightened, flattening the thread. On removal, the width of the thread is compared with a scale supplied with the thread and the clearance is read off directly. Sometimes joint faces leak persistently, even after gasket renewal. The fault will then be traceable to distortion, dirt or burrs. Studs which are screwed into soft metal frequently raise burrs at the point of entry. A quick cure for this is to chamfer the edge of the hole in the part which fits over the stud.

5 **Always check a replacement part with the original one before it is fitted.**

If parts are not marked, and the order for reassembly is not known, a little detective work will help. Look for marks which are due to wear to see if they can be mated. Joint faces may not be identical due to manufacturing errors, and parts which overlap may be stained, giving a clue to the correct position. Most fixings leave identifying marks especially if they were painted over on assembly. It is then easier to decide whether a nut, for instance, has a plain, a spring, or a shakeproof washer under it. All running surfaces become 'bedded' together after long spells of work and tiny imperfections on one part will be found to have left corresponding marks on the other. This is particularly true of shafts and bearings and even a score on a cylinder wall will show on the piston.

6 Checking end float or rocker clearances by feeler gauge may not always give accurate results because of wear. For instance, the rocker tip which bears on a valve stem may be deeply pitted, in which case the feeler will simply be bridging a depression. Thrust washers may also wear depressions in opposing faces to make accurate measurement difficult. End float is then easier to check by using a dial gauge. It is common practice to adjust end play in bearing assemblies, like front hubs with taper rollers, by doing up the axle nut until the hub becomes stiff to turn and then backing it off a little. Do not use this method with ballbearing hubs as the assembly is often preloaded by tightening the axle nut to its fullest extent. If the splitpin hole will not line up, file the base of the nut a little.

Steering assemblies often wear in the straight-ahead position. If any part is adjusted, make sure that it remains free when moved from lock to lock. Do not be surprised if an assembly like a steering gearbox, which is known to be carefully adjusted outside the car, becomes stiff when it is bolted in place. This will be due to distortion of the case by the pull of the mounting bolts, particularly if the mounting points are not all touching together. This problem may be met in other equipment and is cured by careful attention to the alignment of mounting points.

When a spanner is stamped with a size and A/F it means that the dimension is the width between the jaws and has no connection with ANF, which is the designation for the American National Fine thread. Coarse threads like Whitworth are rarely used on cars to-day except for studs which screw into soft aluminium or cast iron. For this reason it might be found that the top end of a cylinder head stud has a fine thread and the lower end a coarse thread to screw into the cylinder block. If the car has mainly UNF threads then it is likely that any coarse threads will be UNC, which are not the same as Whitworth. Small sizes have the same number of threads in Whitworth and UNC, but in the $\frac{1}{2}$ inch size for example, there are twelve threads to the inch in the former and thirteen in the latter.

7 After a major overhaul, particularly if a great deal of work has been done on the braking, steering and suspension systems, it is advisable to approach the problem of testing with care. If the braking system has been overhauled, apply heavy pressure to the brake pedal and get a second operator to check every possible source of leakage. The brakes may work extremely well, but a leak could cause complete failure after a few miles.

Do not fit the hub caps until every wheel nut has been checked for tightness, and make sure the tyre pressures are correct. Check the levels of coolant, lubricants and hydraulic fluids. Being satisfied that all is well, take the car on the road and test the brakes at once. Check the steering and the action of the handbrake. Do all this at moderate speeds on quiet roads, and make sure there is no other vehicle behind you when you try a rapid stop.

Finally, remember that many parts settle down after a time, so check for tightness of all fixings after the car has been on the road for a hundred miles or so.

8 It is useless to tune an engine which has not reached its normal running temperature. In the same way, the tune of an engine which is stiff after a rebore will be different when the engine is again running free. Remember too, that rocker clearances on pushrod operated valve gear will change when the cylinder head nuts are tightened after an initial period of running with a new head gasket.

Trouble may not always be due to what seems the obvious cause. Ignition, carburation and mechanical condition are interdependent and spitting back through the carburetter, which might be attributed to a weak mixture, can be caused by a sticking inlet valve.

For one final hint on tuning, never adjust more than one thing at a time or it will be impossible to tell which adjustment produced the desired result.

NOTES

GLOSSARY OF TERMS

Allen key — Cranked wrench of hexagonal section for use with socket head screws.

Alternator — Electrical generator producing alternating current. Rectified to direct current for battery charging.

Ambient temperature — Surrounding atmospheric temperature.

Annulus — Used in engineering to indicate the outer ring gear of an epicyclic gear train.

Armature — The shaft carrying the windings, which rotates in the magnetic field of a generator or starter motor. That part of a solenoid or relay which is activated by the magnetic field.

Axial — In line with, or pertaining to, an axis.

Backlash — Play in meshing gears.

Balance lever — A bar where force applied at the centre is equally divided between connections at the ends.

Banjo axle — Axle casing with large diameter housing for the crownwheel and differential.

Bendix pinion — A self-engaging and self-disengaging drive on a starter motor shaft.

Bevel pinion — A conical shaped gearwheel, designed to mesh with a similar gear with an axis usually at 90 deg. to its own.

bhp — Brake horse power, measured on a dynamometer.

bmep — Brake mean effective pressure. Average pressure on a piston during the working stroke.

Brake cylinder — Cylinder with hydraulically operated piston(s) acting on brake shoes or pad(s).

Brake regulator — Control valve fitted in hydraulic braking system which limits brake pressure to rear brakes during heavy braking to prevent rear wheel locking.

Camber — Angle at which a wheel is tilted from the vertical.

Capacitor — Modern term for an electrical condenser. Part of distributor assembly, connected across contact breaker points, acts as an interference suppressor.

Castellated — Top face of a nut, slotted across the flats, to take a locking splitpin.

Caster — Angle at which the kingpin or swivel pin is tilted when viewed from the side.

cc — Cubic centimetres. Engine capacity is arrived at by multiplying the area of the bore in sq cm by the stroke in cm by the number of cylinders.

Clevis — U-shaped forked connector used with a clevis pin, usually at handbrake connections.

Collet — A type of collar, usually split and located in a groove in a shaft, and held in place by a retainer. The arrangement used to retain the spring(s) on a valve stem in most cases.

Commutator — Rotating segmented current distributor between armature windings and brushes in generator or motor.

Compression ratio — The ratio, or quantitative relation, of the total volume (piston at bottom of stroke) to the unswept volume (piston at top of stroke) in an engine cylinder.

Condenser — See capacitor.

Core plug — Plug for blanking off a manufacturing hole in a casting.

Crownwheel — Large bevel gear in rear axle, driven by a bevel pinion attached to the propeller shaft. Sometimes called a 'ring gear'.

'C'-spanner — Like a 'C' with a handle. For use on screwed collars without flats, but with slots or holes.

Damper — Modern term for shock-absorber, used in vehicle suspension systems to damp out spring oscillations.

Depression — The lowering of atmospheric pressure as in the inlet manifold and carburetter.

Dowel — Close tolerance pin, peg, tube, or bolt, which accurately locates mating parts.

Drag link — Rod connecting steering box drop arm (pitman arm) to nearest front wheel steering arm in certain types of steering systems.

Dry liner — Thinwall tube pressed into cylinder bore

Dry sump — Lubrication system where all oil is scavenged from the sump, and returned to a separate tank.

Dynamo — See Generator.

Electrode — Terminal, part of an electrical component, such as the points or 'Electrodes' of a sparking plug.

Electrolyte — In lead-acid car batteries a solution of sulphuric acid and distilled water.

End float — The axial movement between associated parts, end play.

EP — Extreme pressure. In lubricants, special grades for heavily loaded bearing surfaces, such as gear teeth in a gearbox, or crownwheel and pinion in a rear axle.

Fade	Of brakes. Reduced efficiency due to overheating.	**Journals**	Those parts of a shaft that are in contact with the bearings.
Field coils	Windings on the polepieces of motors and generators.	**Kingpin**	The main vertical pin which carries the front wheel spindle, and permits steering movement. May be called 'steering pin' or 'swivel pin'.
Fillets	Narrow finishing strips usually applied to interior bodywork.		
First motion shaft	Input shaft from clutch to gearbox.	**Layshaft**	The shaft which carries the laygear in the gearbox. The laygear is driven by the first motion shaft and drives the third motion shaft according to the gear selected. Sometimes called the 'countershaft' or 'second motion shaft.'
Fullflow filter	Filters in which all the oil is pumped to the engine. If the element becomes clogged, a bypass valve operates to pass unfiltered oil to the engine.		
FWD	Front wheel drive.	**lb ft**	A measure of twist or torque. A pull of 10 lb at a radius of 1 ft is a torque of 10 lb ft.
Gear pump	Two meshing gears in a close fitting casing. Oil is carried from the inlet round the outside of both gears in the spaces between the gear teeth and casing to the outlet, the meshing gear teeth prevent oil passing back to the inlet, and the oil is forced through the outlet port.		
		lb/sq in	Pounds per square inch.
		Little-end	The small, or piston end of a connecting rod. Sometimes called the 'small-end'.
		LT	Low Tension. The current output from the battery.
Generator	Modern term for 'Dynamo'. When rotated produces electrical current.	**Mandrel**	Accurately manufactured bar or rod used for test or centring purposes.
Grommet	A ring of protective or sealing material. Can be used to protect pipes or leads passing through bulkheads.	**Manifold**	A pipe, duct, or chamber, with several branches.
		Needle rollers	Bearing rollers with a length many times their diameter.
Grubscrew	Fully threaded headless screw with screwdriver slot. Used for locking, or alignment purposes.		
Gudgeon pin	Shaft which connects a piston to its connecting rod. Sometimes called 'wrist pin', or 'piston pin'.	**Oil bath**	Reservoir which lubricates parts by immersion. In air filters, a separate oil supply for wetting a wire mesh element to hold the dust.
Halfshaft	One of a pair transmitting drive from the differential.	**Oil wetted**	In air filters, a wire mesh element lightly oiled to trap and hold airborne dust.
Helical	In spiral form. The teeth of helical gears are cut at a spiral angle to the side faces of the gearwheel.	**Overlap**	Period during which inlet and exhaust valves are open together.
Hot spot	Hot area that assists vapourisation of fuel on its way to cylinders. Often provided by close contact between inlet and exhaust manifolds.	**Panhard rod**	Bar connected between fixed point on chassis and another on axle to control sideways movement.
		Pawl	Pivoted catch which engages in the teeth of a ratchet to permit movement in one direction only.
HT	High Tension. Applied to electrical current produced by the ignition coil for the sparking plugs.	**Peg spanner**	Tool with pegs, or pins, to engage in holes or slots in the part to be turned.
Hydrometer	A device for checking specific gravity of liquids. Used to check specific gravity of electrolyte.	**Pendant pedals**	Pedals with levers that are pivoted at the top end.
Hypoid bevel gears	A form of bevel gear used in the rear axle drive gears. The bevel pinion meshes below the centre line of the crownwheel, giving a lower propeller shaft line.	**Phillips screwdriver**	A cross-point screwdriver for use with the cross-slotted heads of Phillips screws.
		Pinion	A small gear, usually in relation to another gear.
Idler	A device for passing on movement. A free running gear between driving and driven gears. A lever transmitting track rod movement to a side rod in steering gear.	**Piston-type damper**	Shock absorber in which damping is controlled by a piston working in a closed oil-filled cylinder.
		Preloading	Preset static pressure on ball or roller bearings not due to working loads.
Impeller	A centrifugal pumping element. Used in water pumps to stimulate flow.	**Radial**	Radiating from a centre, like the spokes of a wheel.

Radius rod	Pivoted arm confining movement of a part to an arc of fixed radius.
Ratchet	Toothed wheel or rack which can move in one direction only, movement in the other being prevented by a pawl.
Ring gear	A gear tooth ring attached to outer periphery of flywheel. Starter pinion engages with it during starting.
Runout	Amount by which rotating part is out of true.
Semi-floating axle	Outer end of rear axle halfshaft is carried on bearing inside axle casing. Wheel hub is secured to end of shaft.
Servo	A hydraulic or pneumatic system for assisting, or, augmenting a physical effort. See 'Vacuum Servo'.
Setscrew	One which is threaded for the full length of the shank.
Shackle	A coupling link, used in the form of two parallel pins connected by side plates to secure the end of the master suspension spring and absorb the effects of deflection.
Shell bearing	Thinwalled steel shell lined with anti-friction metal. Usually semi-circular and used in pairs for main and big-end bearings.
Shock absorber	See 'Damper'.
Silentbloc	Rubber bush bonded to inner and outer metal sleeves.
Socket-head screw	Screw with hexagonal socket for an Alien key.
Solenoid	A coil of wire creating a magnetic field when electric current passes through it. Used with a soft iron core to operate contacts or a mechanical device.
Spur gear	A gear with teeth cut axially across the periphery.
Stub axle	Short axle fixed at one end only.
Tachometer	An instrument for accurate measurement of rotating speed. Usually indicates in revolutions per minute.
TDC	Top Dead Centre. The highest point reached by a piston in a cylinder, with the crank and connecting rod in line.
Thermostat	Automatic device for regulating temperature. Used in vehicle coolant systems to open a valve which restricts circulation at low temperature.
Third motion shaft	Output shaft of gearbox.
Threequarter floating axle	Outer end of rear axle halfshaft flanged and bolted to wheel hub, which runs on bearing mounted on outside of axle casing. Vehicle weight is not carried by the axle shaft.
Thrust bearing or washer	Used to reduce friction in rotating parts subject to axial loads.
Torque	Turning or twisting effort. See 'lb ft'.
Track rod	The bar(s) across the vehicle which connect the steering arms and maintain the front wheels in their correct alignment.
UJ	Universal joint. A coupling between shafts which permits angular movement.
UNF	Unified National Fine screw thread.
Vacuum servo	Device used in brake system, using difference between atmospheric pressure and inlet manifold depression to operate a piston which acts to augment brake pressure as required. See 'Servo'.
Venturi	A restriction or 'choke' in a tube, as in a carburetter, used to increase velocity to obtain a reduction in pressure.
Vernier	A sliding scale for obtaining fractional readings of the graduations of an adjacent scale.
Welch plug	A domed thin metal disc which is partially flattened to lock in a recess. Used to plug core holes in castings.
Wet liner	Removable cylinder barrel, sealed against coolant leakage, where the coolant is in direct contact with the outer surface.
Wet sump	A reservoir attached to the crankcase to hold the lubricating oil.

NOTES

INDEX